Don't Make Beats Like Me

Don't Make Beats Like Me

24 Powerful Laws To Guide You
Towards Success As A Music Producer

CHRISTOPHER "MAYDAY" RUCKS

Table of Contents

Contents

ACKNOWLEDGMENTS

THIS BOOK was waiting for me. I never had any intention to write it. That's how things work out when you're prepared, I guess. You've acquired all of the pieces and you don't have a clue there is something to build. Earned an English degree. Strove unsuccessfully to communicate via the language of music, made beats. Became an educator of producers. Connected with some incredibly passionate and authentic individuals. Then I looked up, and magically, all the pieces were lying there in front of me and all I had to do was put them on paper. That's how things work when you're fulfilling your purpose and being of service.

The most critical pieces of that thing you build are the people who help you along the way. The first "thank you" is reserved for my beautiful parents, Al Rucks and Jacqueline White, who have supported me unimaginably throughout this process.

Thank you to: Felisha Booker, Denny Lavish, Kenton Clayton, John Vereen, Sonya M., Brandy O'Neal, Will Tolbert, Focus..., Chuck Greene, REO,

Troy Taylor, Fuego, Ric Spicer and Dia Hodari of Sweatbeatz Productions, Dow and Hen of Tha Bizness, DJ Khalil, Needlz, Dynamic Producer, Jaay Peso, Max Powers, Ed McDonald, Suraj, Vess, Sincere, Chris Cabott, and everyone else who has supported the development of this book. I wouldn't be writing this without all of you. Special thanks to the entire Music Dealers family, past and present, and thank you to those who, with the best of intentions, harassed me until I turned this book in to the publisher, including Jason Bowman, Jude Georgen, John Williamson, Josh Kaplan, and the team at the Chicago Hyde Park Starbucks, who saw me coming in year after year to grind away on it and always asked how it was coming. Thank you to my editor, Catherine Oliver, the editorial forewoman who, draft after draft, thoroughly inspected my house of words, forcing me, with her guidance and encouragement, to rebuild it better, stronger, and more efficiently each time.

To the producers involved with helping me develop this book, and to manager extraordinaire Chuck Greene: I don't think you have any idea what you've done. You've each been instrumental in working with me to create something that the producer culture so desperately needs, and it's right on time. I want to thank you all, once more, for sitting down with me and sharing the best and worst parts of your journeys so I could channel that information and share it with those hoping to rise to the heights you've all been blessed to reach. I know that many producers will thank you for your contributions to this book. I am indebted to each of you.

Thank you everyone!

INTRO

THIS BOOK was conceived from the Law of Karma.

Years ago, I was introduced to a book by Deepak Chopra called *The Seven Spiritual Laws of Success*. Immersed in the book and trying to wrap my mind around the concepts in it, I remember focusing specifically on Law Number 3: The Law of "Karma" or Cause and Effect. It was sometime while reading this chapter that I was struck with the idea to write this book. The ever-wise Deepak Chopra was explaining how we pay our karmic debt by converting our adversity and challenges into a benefit for someone else. He calls this "the transmutation of your karma into a positive experience." I thought about this concept and wondered, "What the hell have *I* experienced that could possibly benefit anyone?" Obviously, it would have to be something close to my heart so the passion would be real. Then, it dawned on me. I had something to give after all: when I was trying to become a producer, I made a ton of mistakes, and they were all based on how I felt and what I was thinking, not on how smart I was or anything external to myself. Now, what could I do with that?

After being laid off from my position as a paralegal, I dedicated my time to video and music production and to educating myself about me so I could get rid of the elements of my personality that were holding me back from maximizing my potential. I became interested in what makes the successful, successful—the great, great—and what drives people *to do* those correct things that bring success and greatness. I was in my mid-twenties, and I was at a point where I was beginning to feel the need to discover my own greatness. I wanted to find my path to success. I knew these things were buried treasures within, but I didn't know how to excavate them. Finding myself with an abundance of time, I had the perfect opportunity to correct whatever course I was on and make sure I found those treasures.

I read through a long list of books to increase my knowledge in the areas of emotional intelligence, psychology, and successful living, and I began to learn that people who find their own treasures of greatness and success have specific ways of speaking to themselves. They know how to conquer their emotions and actions when they're trying to reach a goal.

As the months passed and the books piled up, my knowledge of successful thinking began to increase. During this time of self-discovery, I began working with Dynamic Producer, an organization whose mission is to educate and provide opportunities to aspiring producers. And this was about the time I ran into Chopra's Law of Karma. While fatefully reading that chapter, I began to be able to clearly trace back the majority of the suspect actions and stupid mistakes I'd made as an aspiring producer, clearly understanding what had been going on in my mind at that time. And as I was molding this thought Play-Doh in my head, I realized that as a guy who was then interacting with and watching the grind of dozens of producers at a time, I saw many of the producers and beatmakers around me *making the very same mistakes*. It was like watching my own failures being sampled, then looped on "repeat" over and over again. Even today, working at Music Dealers, a music agency and sync licensing company, I see more of the same—up-and-coming creators of music who are victims of their own poor thinking, which leads to their own suspect actions and stupid mistakes.

That's how I decided I was going to "transmute my karma into a positive experience" and use my own adversity to serve someone else. I realized that when you're out there grinding away, working and slaving toward your goal, it's hard as hell to step back and make sure you're being the "you" that you need to be to create success as a producer. Knowing this truth, I really just wanted to help.

When I started writing this book, I knew that I was blessed with a point of view afforded to few people. There has always been only a handful of organizations around the country committed to providing knowledge and opportunities to aspiring music producers. And of those few organizations, few of their leaders had sat in front of a program or a drum machine, day after day, with the goal of organizing sounds into music that other people enjoyed. Few of these producer leaders and educators understood deeply the joy and pain of climbing the high staircase toward success as a producer. I understood that climb. When I started writing this book, the aches in my legs were still very fresh from it. I understood the failures associated with it. And by unexpectedly finding myself as an educator of producers, I knew I could help as many producers as possible avoid the traps that do just enough daily damage to hold them back from achieving success. I had lived it.

Now that you understand the birth of this book and know that I'm not some clown writing to stroke his ego at the sight of his name appearing on Amazon.com, allow me to explain what this book is and is not.

This book is not about production techniques. Those subjects are touched upon, but we're not here to dive deeply into drum programming and track sequencing. They are mentioned, but our focus isn't on creating rich sounds and writing memorable progressions and melodies. Today, you can get a solid hold of that stuff with a single YouTube search. However, few people on YouTube are going to address how *you as a person* fits into your success as a music producer. It's because of that lack of insight that I've written a book for *you*, about *you*—the most important piece of equipment in your studio. Everything you do as a creator of music and an aspiring producer starts from your thoughts and emotions—from the mind all decisions flow; you are your thoughts. What makes this so ridiculously important? Production techniques and equipment always change; however, the way you think, well, *that can last your whole damn career*. It doesn't matter how talented you are; if your thinking is faulty, you'll fail. If your thinking is substandard, your career will be, too. If your mind isn't right, nothing will be. This is why you're reading this.

Each chapter in this book is based on a law, but abiding by these laws isn't about how smart you are. You may have just been in the middle of thinking, "I'm a smart dude; I don't have to worry about this stuff." Think again. I'm a smart guy, too. I always did well in school, graduated with a strong GPA from a good college, and communicated effectively. I thought I was a sharp cat. But my own production career had little to do with my intellect. During my short journey as a producer, from the winter of 2004 to the summer or fall of 2008 (I resurrected and produced for fun in 2010 and 2011), I rarely used logic or my so-called intellect to make decisions. In fact, I hardly ever used my analytical side to make decisions. I made train-wreck decisions based on unreliable emotions, like most of the world does. What were some of the traits that steered my mental train wreck? Fear, lack of courage, too much pride, inadequate confidence, an overactive ego, impatience, insufficient desire, a poor belief system, greed, and a few others. When all of them combined like Voltron to work against me, they took a sledgehammer to my chances to succeed as a producer. Any of us can succumb.

Our emotions, thoughts, and habits govern the majority of moves we make as human beings. And guess what? When we're creative people, struggling to birth dope art, it's even worse. Poor thinking can grab your potential, strangle the life out of your progress, and leave your possibilities a limp, lifeless mass of what-should-have-been. I'm going to try to help you avoid that. Instead, within this book you'll find a recipe for success by properly interlocking your rational mind and emotional mind, then making the right decisions and aligning them with relentless action. This is about giving you the knowledge to make you grind smarter and harder. With a lifetime of collective wisdom and experience to pull from, when we're done here, you're going to be razor-sharp and feel motivated like you never have before. I guarantee that.

I can also tell you this: I am not "the man." The production world does not look up to me for my music. I don't have Platinum plaques adorning the walls in my halls. Hell, I barely had any MCs rap over my beats. This book is about why all of those things couldn't exist for me. But by walking in your shoes—working, tweaking, evolving, and sacrificing day after day—and thoroughly examining my failures, I can tell you what *not* to do. I can tell you all of the silly decisions I made regarding my music, especially having been in a position to eyeball producers who do the same things I did. After reading and absorbing this book, you'll be able to avoid many of the false paths before you. The more roads you know to avoid, the more opportunities you'll have to take the right ones.

Let me tell you what else this book is. It's a deep look into production success—a look into the souls of people who've conquered what you hope to conquer. My own wisdom isn't enough; for this journey, you'll need much more. When I first got started making beats, I would have killed for the chance to speak and politic with producers who created music I loved. As I moved to the business side of things, I got that opportunity. So I reached out to some of the producers who do what you dream of doing, who live how you one day hope to live, who've found a way to wake up every morning and do what they love—produce music—and love where they've managed to put themselves.

I want you to also know this: I didn't sit down and spend hours speaking with just anybody. I specifically chose people who were authentic. I spoke to successful producers who knew they had to share their truth, not a fabricated version of how they got where they are, filled with rainbows and fairy dust and unicorns. They shared their joys and successes, their heartbreaks and failures. Not everyone is built to openly discuss the things I asked about. Recognize that these are special people. And speaking with me for this book is a part of their vision and desire to give back to our culture. They understand that as crazy and fragmented as the production community is, it's their community, and they want to spread the knowledge to those of you fighting every day to get where they are. You're about to receive profound wisdom from:

- **DJ Khalil,** Platinum seller, Grammy winner (production credits include 50 Cent, Jay-Z, Eminem, Game, Aloe Blacc)
- **Needlz,** Platinum seller, Grammy winner (production credits include Bruno Mars, Drake, Young Jeezy, Lupe Fiasco)
- **Troy Taylor,** Platinum seller, Grammy winner (production credits include Trey Songz, the Isley Brothers, Tyrese, Stevie Wonder, SWV, Whitney Houston)
- **Chuck Greene** (co-manager of J.U.S.T.I.C.E. League, Platinum sellers, Grammy winners)

- **Focus…,** Platinum seller, Grammy winner (production credits include Beyoncé, Schoolboy Q, Game, Busta Rhymes)
- **REO,** Platinum seller (production credits include Chris Brown, Big Sean, Leona Lewis, Beyoncé)
- **Tha Bizness,** Platinum sellers, Grammy winners (production credits include Lil Wayne, Young Jeezy, Chris Brown, Kendrick Lamar)

These producers have been in the game for *years.* I purposely didn't speak to anyone too fresh or suddenly in the headlines as that so-called "it" guy because I know that *becoming* a producer eventually develops into *trying to maintain* producer status. The wisdom from these producers isn't about getting in, getting hot, and disappearing. Their insight comes from being blessed with careers. Look beyond mere words and quotes on a page.

I tried to design this book so that reading it feels like you're sharing a favorite drink with a close friend, bellied up to the weathered wood and brass bar of an old lounge (you young-'uns, just use your imagination). You sip slowly, leaning upon the shiny, finished slab of wood before you. Billowing tufts of aromatic cigar smoke dance in the air. You lean in to cut through the volume of the chatter around you, making sure no word escapes. As the bartender pours drinks, this friend pours experiences—bitter failures and joyous victories—in a way that allows you to ride the ups and downs of his journey like waves on a sea.

Don't Make Beats Like Me is divided into four sections. Part 1 explores the internal resources you will absolutely need to cultivate success. It may feel like a gut check, but it's necessary to prepare you for the rest of the book. Part 2 focuses on several obstacles that producers create for themselves on their way to eventually becoming their own worst enemies. Part 3 begins to move from the interior to the exterior by examining how our thinking affects us as we deal with the external world of production. In Part 4, we'll examine your production habits and actions, like networking, craft mastery, and the way you conduct business—all direct descendants of your thinking.

Each part of the book is composed of laws. Most laws are based on a critical error I made as an aspiring producer. A few laws near the end of the book are based on the occasional wise decision. Most of the book's laws will begin with observations, designed to help paint a picture of the error made, followed by realizations, which will analyze mistakes, discuss the costs of those mistakes, and provide advice and wisdom to overcome them. Final mixes will leave with you with a concluding thought or a last word of wisdom before you move on to the next law.

I've woven the wisdom from the producers interviewed throughout the book like a DJ would scratch vocal samples into a beat, supplementing the laws, giving them tested, real-world legitimacy. Some laws are brief, but potent. Others deal with much heavier subjects and need more analysis. Yet each one is important—just because you haven't yet experienced a law doesn't mean it won't unexpectedly photobomb the picture of your career.

Finally, this book was written because so few have written anything for music producers. We have few tools to carry in our back pockets and pull out when we need a word of inspiration or guidance on a particular decision. You can buy a self-help book on losing weight, finding love, landing a great job, getting out of debt, or being a rapper, but what do we producers have, especially considering how difficult our journey is? Earning and maintaining production success is a goddamn Herculean task. Our industry is another industry's nightmare. You need as much wisdom as possible to keep yourself walking forward when the entertainment world has its foot on your neck. So this is my purpose: as long as there are topics to cover and questions to answer, I'll be writing books to cover those topics and answer those questions until my fingers ache with arthritis. My failure will be your success. My defeat will be your victory.

Part 1: What Do I Need?

LAW 1

Eyes Wide Open: Know What You Want and What It Costs to Get It

People are always gonna tell you what you can't do. This is a dream, and everybody's gonna tell you that you can't do it: "You'll never be like Kanye West, you'll never be like Just Blaze, you'll never get in the game and do what a Quincy Jones has done." —Chuck Greene, 1 Shot Management

I knew when I was eight years old that I was gonna be a professional producer. That's what I was saying from second or third grade all the way until I graduated. That was my dream since I was a baby. There was nothing in me that was gearing me up to be anything else. I knew I was gonna be a producer, there was no question about it. —Focus...

OBSERVATION

SO, LET'S DIVE right into some necessary steps, starting with this one: *"Decide what you want, decide what you are willing to exchange for it."* Billionaire H. L. Hunt provided this honest response when asked about his ability to accomplish the great things he'd achieved throughout his lifetime.

One thing I never did during my time as a beat-maker was to sit down early in my career and figure out what I wanted from production and what I was willing to exchange for it. Asking myself "What do I want?" would have been like pulling out a map and a compass. I would have given myself the benefit of identifying where I was as a beatmaker, and then I could have outlined a path to where I wanted to go and determined what it was going to take to get there. Instead, I just made these vague declarations about wanting to work with Nas and Ghostface and believed that my production dreams would miraculously materialize.

The second mistake I made was not adequately preparing myself for the sacrifices that each step on that path would require. I think many of us just catch the production bug, and it's so powerfully captivating, we immediately begin making beats. We invest in the music with the fullness of our souls and beings, and somewhere along the way, we just assume that the goals we imagine will magically come to be. We say, "I'm going to get a Jay-Z placement," or we say, "I'm not stopping until I work with Justin Timberlake." But at some point, you have to question what *really* goes into achieving that milestone. What will it take?

What exactly is your dream? Do you see a career in your vision, or is this a hobby? Do you want to thrive from full-time production, or do you just want a few album placements? Do you want to be on the radio, or are you comfortable with album cuts? Is it pop that you're interested in or EDM? Have you thought about film and TV placements? How are you going to get to these destinations? Only when you are honest and certain about what you want can you begin to clarify what you'll have to do to get it.

For example, producing a number-one single for a pop diva would be an incredible accomplishment. It's also a completely different journey, with different milestones, than getting an album placement for a regional rapper. Let's say your dream is to produce a Rihanna record. She's the one artist you'd give your right arm to work with. Do you want an album cut or would you love to get a single? Do you have any idea how skilled you're going to need to be to work with an artist like Rihanna? Do you know what kind of accomplishments or major cosigns you're going to need before someone from her camp entrusts *you* with a song? That album would be a multimillion-dollar investment. Each one of those songs is of considerable value to everyone on that team. Do you know what kind of circles you're going to have to network into to gain that opportunity? The milestones that you'd have to hit are significant.

Have you visualized the necessary steps to get to your own destination? For this example, maybe you intern at Rihanna's label and meet key people while you're building your skills. Maybe you lace lesser-known artists with dope songs in the meantime and someone from her A&R crew takes notice. Maybe you actively seek out and work with some of her past songwriters. Maybe you license music to pay your bills while you're working on these other things. You still have to eat and pay bills, right? These are the kinds of middle steps you have to keep in mind once you set an ambitious goal like that. Now read that again.

For this particular scenario, you would have to:

- Move to where Rihanna's label is located for an internship;
- Master your craft to the point that people are taking notice;
- Not only master your craft, but know the specific skills behind producing urban/pop/R&B records;
- Network your ass off, and network into some of the inner circles that are tough to crack;
- Work with up-and-coming artists to publicize your brand;
- Be prolific enough to set aside a volume of tracks to send out for licensing in TV and film so that the publishing can help support you;
- Learn to work with songwriters effectively and develop not only good records but also great chemistry with those writers who've written for Rihanna and who just might walk some of the work you've done together right through the door to her; and
- Maintain your enthusiasm and passion amid challenges, defeats, missed opportunities, and the passage of time.

REALIZATION

See, when I'm listening to you as you tell me you want to be a boss in the game, respected and admired, I don't hear what you just told me; I hear the steps in between where you are and where you want to be. I know what you may not have realized: that your ability to be a boss is directly related to your ability to conquer the multitude of steps in the middle.

This is one of the most important things I will tell you: *Don't set a vision for yourself and bullshit the daily detailed steps needed to achieve it.* You can't be a successful producer and not do on a daily basis what successful producers do. I want you to realize that the space between where you are and where you'd like to be is critical, and it needs your direct attention. It comprises so many factors, such as time, patience, and extraordinary sacrifice. This thing you love cannot be taken for granted. If you have any misconceptions regarding the goal of producing, I'll be removing them.

Sacrifice

Decide what you are willing to exchange for it. Sacrifice. You can't talk about becoming a producer without talking about sacrifice. I've seen producers spend ten-plus years grinding without any significant success. I've seen cats on the brink of starvation, without two nickels to rub together, beards scruffy, their stomachs rumbling like 808s. These guys would rather buy juicy drums or a new piece of equipment than a juicy steak. You could pack clothes into duffel bags under the eyes of beatmakers who work a nine-to-five and then come home and make beats into the wee hours of the morning.

But I've also seen those who knew what they wanted, who wanted it badly enough, who sacrificed and paid the price, and found what they were seeking. There's no way to tell how long it will take to get your hit or significant placement. Your hard work and struggle could pay off next month or four years from now. There's no definite way to know how much time it will take for publishing checks to sustain you full time. There's a strong element of chance in production, as with many other things in life, and you must properly assess whether you're ready to play the game of chess with the entertainment world. If you want what I think you want, then remember: *This is not for the faint of heart, the squeamish, or the impatient.* You're gonna need to be tougher than woodpecker lips to ball in this arena. Music production is not the business to have delusions of grandeur about.

I remember Needlz tweeting about the frustration and difficulty involved in raising his children and being attentive to his wife and producing full time. And this brother has had an amazing career, with multiple placements and with shiny plaques decorating his walls. His tweet gives you a window into the challenging struggle for balance in production. Would you be willing to sacrifice your family time to master your craft and achieve what Needlz has achieved? Whether you're in the middle of your career or just beginning, sit down now and figure out what your destination is and what you're willing to sacrifice to get to it. Do you *really* want to play?

If you do, then you've got to pay. Some producers invest in themselves monetarily by shelling out thousands of dollars to buy expensive equipment and software, to attend conferences and seminars, and to take music lessons. Some producers invest time and sacrifice their social lives while relentlessly working on their craft. On Friday night, while the world is out in the clubs partying to the hits, dedicated producers are at home, trying to make some.

Some producers move away from friends, loved ones, and family to unfamiliar territory to get it popping. We all remember Kanye's story of packing up his life and moving to Jersey to further his career. It's hard to move your career forward when you live in North-of-Nowhere, Nebraska. Building relationships with check-writers is easier if you live in one of the cities where the business is shaking. Would you be willing to move across a country, continent, or ocean to follow your dream? Does victory mean that much to you?

Some producers put off love, marriage, and children until they can get their careers to a certain level. That can be a lonely lifestyle, which could go on for years. Is that for you? It's more challenging to maintain momentum when you have responsibilities to a spouse or children or both. Your partner needs time, the kids need time, the baby needs diapers, and the family needs food in the fridge. It's not always the easiest thing to put grub on the table and diapers on Junior's bottom when you're waiting on production money. Can you stay focused through those difficult moments and keep moving in the present to make things happen in the future?

Hen, of the Grammy-winning production duo Tha Bizness, had this to say about his and his production partner Dow's personal sacrifices for production success:

> We've put it all on the line, from our relationships, our lifestyles, our health, to our finances, to our credit scores, to whatever. Whatever we gotta do, we have to keep going, you know, and eventually, where we're at now, it's a good place, *even though it's never going to stop*.

Dow chimed in with:

> You just gotta be willing to sacrifice everything, or the most that you can, for what you believe. Shit, most of the people that have made it, they made it because they've damn near given up everything [for] their dream, [for] what they believed in.

That's where you get the motivation to keep doing it, [because] you're looking at everything that you've given up. All the times when we could have been out kicking it with our friends and having fun, we were inside trying to get better at what we do, or we were going somewhere trying to get better at what we do. So ... it's a constant sacrifice. That's life. If everything was free and easy, shit, everyone would be popping.

Breathe deeply those words. They're a true glimpse into the reality of this passion.

Chuck Greene, co-CEO of 1 Shot Management and part of the management team of Grammy-winning, Platinum-plus producers J.U.S.T.I.C.E. League, confirms what the pursuit of this dream can cost:

[I've seen] everything, man. Losing significant others, losing relationships with parents ("You gotta get a real job!"), losing the ability to spend time with your kids, because this demands that kid-time. *It's a heavy cost, [but] it's a heavy reward if you can make it.*

Truer words regarding this journey were never spoken.

I spoke with Focus... (hereinafter, "Focus," without the ellipsis) about what he's sacrificed to achieve his own dreams. He stated:

I pay prices. I have two sons with a woman in California. I didn't get to really be the at-home dad that I wanted to be with them, and that really bothers me more than it bothers them because they know that Dad was working his butt off to make sure they were provided for. But at the end of the day, being there, giving them the time, is more precious than anything. My wife now, I almost lost her behind grinding and staying in the music and making the music more of a priority than her, so I wouldn't have had my daughter. I put myself in a place where I wanted to be so legendary, so important, that I let everything that was important to me fall off and slack.

Not only do these quotes provide you with a clear picture of what real sacrifice looks like, but they also speak about how challenging, yet important, it is to try to maintain some kind of balance between your personal life and your work life. REO, of The Sound-killers, reflected on his own experiences with balance as a producer:

I think another difficult part is balancing a family, a life. You become a recluse, in the studio, just with your headphones on. It's just you and the music. I know a lot of dudes that are in relationships with girls that [are] like, "You're never around, and you never make time for me," you know, and I think that that's really hard to juggle because music is such a personal thing.

I asked Troy Taylor, a respected Platinum-selling writer and producer, about his greatest sacrifices. High on his list was everything he had to give up to stay true to himself in an industry where being true to oneself is not the norm.

> I paid the price of not being cool, not being the who's of who, not being in people's faces and at everybody's party taking a bunch of pictures. I paid the price of simply [not being] cool. But I'm relevant, still, not trendy.

Choosing to remain true to himself meant foregoing the parties, the women, the drugs, the alcohol, the clubs, the trends, and the materialism that are often part of the music industry. He recognized that by excluding himself from those activities, he wouldn't be able to capitalize on the perception of coolness and he'd lose the ability to market himself by attending those kinds of events and taking part in those kinds of activities. Troy was willing to forfeit the benefit of "industry publicity," vowing to be *fully recognized based on his art and talent*, not because he was in the pictures, at the party, or in the studio with a "fresh pair of Gucci shoes," as he put it.

Ask yourself beforehand: *What price am I willing to pay for this passion?* You don't want to suddenly find yourself shocked by the difficulty of pursuing this dream. Answering that question allows you to prepare for what's coming. Then, instead of throwing your hands into the air in frustration—pissed, angry, complaining—you already know that you just might have to wade through a pool of shit to get to your dream at the other end. You minimize energy wasted on being angry and defeated, and instead pour that energy back into becoming the producer you want to be.

Direction, sacrifice, balance—these are the things I never took into consideration when I started producing. No one was there to tell me it was going to take all of *that* to get to the destination I saw in my imagination. Maybe I would have gotten my act together and dug deeper had I known. That's the purpose of this law; I'm that someone for you.

As I conclude this section, please understand that what I don't want to inspire with this chapter is fear. If you feel fear, let that fear inspire deliberate action. Let the fear of realizing you've got more to pay encourage you to do more. Let the fear from the realization that you might not achieve your goals if you don't reach deeper inside of yourself spur true dedication. I made my fair share of sacrifices to produce, but after learning from and listening to the conviction in the voices of successful producers, I'm positive I didn't pay nearly enough. And I never decided what I wanted or truthfully analyzed what it was going to take to be a successful producer. This will be the first time of many that you'll read this: Avoid my mistake, and *don't make beats like me.* Use this chapter to gain the dose of reality you're going to need to succeed.

Producers make it every day. If you conquer all the obstacles I discuss in this book, then, as Chuck Greene says, "If it hits, bro, the payoff is big. All around the board, it's a life-changing situation, and it changes [everything]." And anybody who pays the price can hit. The thing that keeps the music business spinning on its axis is this: we're all just one hit away. Where there's great sacrifice, there's the potential for great reward. Always hold the vision of the possibilities and rewards in your mind. Your vision and passion are what will carry you through when you're sacrificing and you're meeting those milestones on the way to your dreams.

Lastly, although looking at the big picture is essential in any endeavor, never get too rigidly locked into your own path. You have to be fluid; sometimes the road you have planned and the road that's planned for you don't look the same. Keep your eyes open for opportunities you wouldn't expect.

DJ Khalil related the story of how he gained four placements on Eminem's *Recovery* album. He had an opportunity to work with the newly formed group Slaughterhouse. Providing them with tracks wasn't in his immediate plan, and the budget for the work wasn't within his normal rates, but he decided to take a chance on it because he believed in their music. Khalil's track became a single, and the rock-infused hip-hop track was precisely the style that Eminem was looking for.

If Khalil had stuck to a strict plan and ignored a project he believed in creatively, he wouldn't have opened the door to getting several placements on the album of the highest-selling rap artist since Billboard started charting rap. Perhaps we could argue that he was doing exactly what he was supposed to do. We can't say. What we can say is that you must consider all the options and stay vigilant for opportunities that may develop outside of your original plan. You never know how a decision you make will unfold. Know the road, know the goals, but be flexible in how they're met.

THE FINAL MIX

In regard to the rest of the chapters in this book, I understand that it's impossible to put all producers in the same box. So many of you will reside in different places in your careers. Some of you will have mastered some of these concepts, but be completely behind the curve in other areas. Feel free to jump around, absorb the laws that resonate with you, and use them to better yourself and increase your chances of winning. There's something here for everyone, from amateur to professional.

The information I'm giving you here is based on my experiences and the cumulative wisdom of the people I know, observe, and speak with. But there's no single way to become a producer. For example, there are people who don't ever figure out what they want but still end up with a fantastic production career.

So you have to consider that, too. Therefore, when you're reading this book, make sure what I have to say makes sense for you. If you know you want to get somewhere as a producer, and that somewhere has respect and longevity attached to it, then it's probably a good idea to figure out what that means for you and how you're going to do it.

As well, it's tough for me to suggest how much you should sacrifice. I was speaking to a friend who runs a popular production blog and he was telling me that he's careful about what he says because he knows he's in a position of influence and never wants to give out the wrong information. So, yes, you absolutely will need to go at this like a maniac, but I believe in being rational, being objective, and keeping options and opportunities on deck. A career in production won't work out for everyone, and you want to be able to pivot should the situation not look appealing or favorable.

When we're extremely driven toward accomplishing a dream, we can lose sight of what levels of sacrifice are appropriate. Try to maintain balance when it comes to your children, your spouse, and your ability to put food on the table. These are difficult things to talk about, and I want you to know that I'm considering them all and trying to be as responsible as possible with my voice.

Side Note: Start Now

I need to change direction briefly to address anyone using this book as a pair of binoculars to survey the production business before you start the process of making music. If you are well into the process, you can skip to the next chapter. If, however, you are just beginning your journey, or you've been thinking about taking the dive into producing and beatmaking, then make sure you read this section.

I made a costly, costly error in my production career! I can remember the mistake like it was yesterday. I had just landed on the campus of the University of Michigan as a freshman, adjusting to life in a massive dorm, complete with a long hallway of tiny concrete rooms and grisly carpeting. I was housed on the fifth floor, and I remember walking some of the other hallways to see what lovely young co-eds I was sharing my living space with. During my investigations, I was strolling through the third-floor hallways when I heard someone playing a famous Bob James song, "Nautilus," which, thanks to my father, I knew to be the incredible original sample for Ghostface's "Daytona 500." The guy playing "Nautilus" was a producer named Eddie Bronco (who years later would become key to helping me develop my sample game). He was chilling in his dorm room with his turntables, MPC 2000, and record collection, making beats.

Now, I know I'd always been attracted to beats and instrumentals, but it *did not* dawn on me to sit there and investigate the magical process taking place in this dude's dorm room. That MPC looked extremely confusing, and the whole process seemed so technical that I immediately decided it was too difficult for me to bother with. "Look at all those damn buttons! What the hell am I gonna do with that?" So, I stopped outside the room to listen, went in to briefly introduce myself and chop it up with him, and then foolishly kept it moving.

Yo! Can you imagine what would have happened if I'd let intrigue take over and hadn't nonchalantly dismissed the possibility that I could learn to do what he was doing? What in God's name could have been possible if I had simply uttered six words: "So, how do you do this?" What kind of crazy records could I have been producing right now if I had *not* sold myself short?

I would have had a four-year head start on my production process. All those free moments I spent in college being unproductive could have gone to perfecting the craft, and I would have been *nice*! Not only that, but right under my nose, on the college campus, there was a vast network of beatmakers and producers that I didn't learn of until four years later, when I finally started making beats. The advantages in that environment would have been amazing. I had access to mentors, record stores, and piano lessons from students in the music school, and I had plenty of time with minimal responsibilities! *Start now.* If you're moved by the art, investigate it. Ask someone for some insight. Watch them make music. If you're curious, follow your curiosity, and see what wonderful places it can take you. The longer you wait to start, the longer it will take to get *nice.* Point-blank. In production, you're working against Father Time, just as with any other craft that requires daily practice to reach a high skill level.

I've encountered my fair share of dreamers who talk endlessly about making beats but never seem to take the plunge. They say, "Yo, I would flip this, and I would sample that." "Yo, I love producers and beatmakers." "I'm gonna start my own production company, man. It's gonna be nuts!" Flapping of the gums means nothing until I hear a melody, a kick, and a snare. Personally, I don't want to hear anything about "starting" or "trying" to make beats. Go get FL Studio or something like Reason, some headphones, and a midi controller, download some drums, and be on your way. The people who are always talking about starting never start. The ones who mean it have just come back from Guitar Center with all their equipment and are calling up another producer, asking how to use a DAW. If you mean it, get cracking.

LAW 2

Beyond Desire: Determine If You Have Enough Hunger for the Journey Ahead

You gotta love it. Do you wake up and think about music? — Needlz

OBSERVATION

Desire. What does desire look like? What does desire feel like?

Being on the opposite side of the producer movement, I've gotten a chance to see what a producer's desire looks like. I can hear desire in the voice of people who really have it. I didn't have the proper amount of desire to become a full-fledged producer, something I realized as I was putting together this book. I had *some,* but not enough to give myself a shot at success. And maybe you're operating under the same misconception that you're full of desire when you actually have only a meager amount of what you'll need to succeed. That misconception could be disastrous.

Your desire must be relentless. Those with relentless desire never stop improving and pushing the boundaries of their skills. Those with desire find mentors;

they hunt people down and don't take no for an answer. They hang around studios, doing whatever's required of them to get the opportunity to learn from master craftsmen. Eternally obsessed with improvement, they humble themselves to become better, avoiding the trap of sitting back and resting, believing they are "there." There is no "there" in production. There is always more to do or create—more memorable melodies, better drum programming. "Better, more, stronger, quicker" is the successful producer's mantra.

Desire is out in the streets. He's in your face at the show, saying, "I've got songs and tracks." Desire knows where the artists and A&Rs he wants to work with will be. He puts his fear of networking behind him, musters the courage to stop a manager or an attorney who looks like a complete and total asshole, and makes an impression. He conquers the fear of having that man look at him like he's out of his flipping mind. Then he does it again and again. Desire won't quit. He knows he's got product, and he does whatever it takes to make sure his target knows exactly who he is and what he's got.

Desire moves away from home if he needs to. He makes a way to move to where the action is in his genre. If he can't move, he finds a way to get away for a weekend, a week, a month—whatever it takes so he can track down his targets and get in the studio. Desire doesn't give a flying 747 f*ck about red tape. Desire keeps a pair of scissors with him to cut through that bull. I've seen people with ridiculous desire cut through politics and tape and make a way to the studio. This is what real desire does. Desire knows that if he can't find his target artist, he's finding that person's assistant or intern, homeboy, weed toter, or bodyguard. And he's getting in the studio with them because the word may spread.

Desire doesn't care what it will cost. If it helps him improve his sound, he's saving his money and he's getting it. If he can sample, arrange, compose, and mix in the same place, and it will save him time and allow him to boost his creativity, he's copping that program. He's not buying drinks at the bar. He's not pissing away his software money at the local strip club. Desire must have his equipment. Desire has someone teaching him the keys. Desire takes a music theory course. Or he finds a way to get someone to play the keys for him if it will make the end product better. Why? Because he wants it. He wants it so badly he'll do whatever it takes.

He'll stay in a studio lobby for forty-eight hours straight—musty, funky, washing up in the studio bathroom—because he knows that a few of his target artists record there. If that magical question just happens to get asked—"Who's got beats?"—he's right there with disc in hand. Desire knows there are a million producers out there, but he doesn't give a damn. He's going to make it. Everything else is just background noise. If there's a beat battle and someone key is judging, he's entering, and he's introducing himself to everyone of importance afterward, getting their opinion and creating a pathway to make contact again. Desire makes adjustments to the game plan. If it's slow and it isn't working, he recognizes the situation and finds another way. Desire doesn't keep doing the same thing over and over, not learning from mistakes. Desire acknowledges, adjusts, and progresses.

REALIZATION

Don't make beats like me. I never obtained *this* level of desire, and I had no idea until years later. Instead, I wallowed in frustration without knowing why. Yes, I was infatuated with music and creating and the spirit of production and beats. It was love at first sight. Unfortunately, I didn't couple that love with the kind of *relentless* desire that makes you do the work that you don't want to do. I didn't reach beyond the cute and fuzzy surface charm of production and pull out the kind of desire required to achieve significant success.

Dragging myself to events I had no interest in attending, to network with the right people, sticking it out to see if long shots bloomed into opportunities—

I thought these things were beneath me. I missed out. I kept my mouth shut when I should have been speaking. I gave up too easily. Desire must be your constant partner in crime, because when you're unsure, scared, tired, and nervous, desire is there, ready to speak. Desire is there to do. When you're ready to give up, desire is there to forge ahead and drag your ass with it.

You get a rude awakening every once in a while when you come across someone else's desire. When you read or hear about the guy who packed up and moved with five bucks in his pocket because he wanted to work with a certain producer or company. Or when you hear about the woman who almost went homeless in pursuit of her desire to become a song-writer and eventually succeeded. What about the guy who had three dollars a day for food and slept on the floor of a studio apartment for four or five years until he could get his business off the ground? Then it dawns on you: "Damn, they've got desire. They want it. I would never do that!" For some, the reality of true desire sticks, while for others, they forget the wake-up call, hit the snooze button, and revert to their half-assed desire. I did this. Many of us do. This is the difference between regular desire and *relentless* desire—the kind of desire that turns the awful, the impossible, and the undoable into just another hurdle on the way to the goal.

What's beautiful about desire is that it applies to anything and everything. I'm speaking about this in the context of being a producer, but it doesn't matter what aim you're striving for. It's a necessary component for success, an integral piece of the pie. *But let me tell you what's so damn scary about desire.* You can think you have it, but not really have it. You can swear that you desire a thing, an outcome, or a position. You *do* desire it. But you don't quite desire it enough to get nice and uncomfortable. You don't desire it enough to overpower the other parts of yourself that doubt, that fear. And as a result, there are things you don't do and *won't do.* There are things that you overlook and miss because you don't have enough desire to step way out beyond your comfort zone to acquire what you seek. *But you don't know that you don't know.* That's terrifying!

THE FINAL MIX

I want to give you an idea of what desire looks like from the people who've obviously harnessed and used it to build their careers. Troy Taylor says:

> [Desire means] sticking through it, and that seems like a simple answer, but it's not, because sticking through it means you're still moving forward. I've been in situations where I left my company of twelve years. I started from scratch, *jumped off the cliff blindfolded, not knowing if there's gonna be*

any safety nets. That was an act of me saying that I wanna do this. I'm so wanting to do this that I'm willing to leave my comfort zone to get there. Comfort zones simply mean a thing that holds you back, keeps you in one spot, in one place, [not] being willing to leave it to explore a new zone. Most people don't like to leave their comfort zone because they're not familiar with what lies ahead. So they stay where they are.

Jumping off a cliff and not knowing if there'll be a safety net is a perfect metaphor for this business. I asked Dow of Tha Bizness what desire is to him. His answer: "[Desire looks like] the dude who learns how to manage off of two to four hours of sleep because, shit, he works the regular nine-to-five and then he tries to figure out how to do his beats from five to nine." Are you the kind of cat who's willing to sacrifice a good night's sleep every evening to work in as much craft-mastering time as possible?

Focus also shared his vision of desire:

It's unfortunate, but desire equals sacrifice to me, if you're willing to make the sacrifices that *are* needed, not the sacrifices that you *might think are needed.* You might have to sacrifice doing what you want for doing what you have to do. You might want to go out with your boys and go clubbing, or you might want to just sit around with your girl and watch movies, but you need to be perfecting your craft.

...When I see the sweat on a cat's brow, that's what desire looks like to me. When I see a cat kind of antsy, rubbing his palms together, and his palms are sweaty because he's really worried about what cats are gonna think about his music, that's desire. When I see [them] say, "Yo, I can't believe I'm actually here!" … that's desire.

Now there're so many people that think they're the shit already, and you can't tell 'em nothing. That ain't desire. That's just a cat that has a good ego, and he could probably sell you on the fact that he's got some bomb beats, but it's all about showing and proving. So my picture of desire is that nervous young-'un that really still has heart and *really wants to make a difference with his music.*

Desire equals sacrifice? That sounds very familiar.

Not only will you need burning desire, but you'll need to apply that burning desire to different stages in your career. As Chuck Greene puts it, "The desire to be in anything and the desire to stay in anything— if you don't have those two, you'll make it in, but you'll fizzle out." When describing what desire meant to him, Chuck emphasized the importance of your desire's being strong enough to fuel your ascent to becoming a producer, as well as your ability to maintain and improve your position once achieved. As I mentioned before, production is a two-part process.

Focus, in agreement with Chuck, said:

Becoming is always a grind. Where I come from, we always paid our dues. That was difficult in itself, but now maintaining your name seems to be just as hard as becoming a name, especially with the climate of the music and the way these cats are just coming out of the woodwork—these makeshift producers—and they make you obsolete. I think it's pretty much neck-and-neck because I feel like I'm on the same exact grind now that I was [on] when I was trying to get heard. You have to work to get there, and you have to want to keep working to stay there.

I've been in the unusual position of watching the lives and hearing the stories of dozens of producers at one time. When I see someone who wants to become a professional producer, who has a ridiculous amount of desire, that individual stands out. So, ask yourself, "Do I desire that which I seek? Am I sure?" At some point, some of us who want beautiful things from life eventually fall off the wagon and settle into what's here and available instead of pursuing what we really want. The dreams of youth become the regrets of maturity, as they say. Make sure your desire is sufficient, not just for the world of music production but for anything, or the regrets may come to haunt you. Those who want it long and hard enough will do whatever it takes to eventually get it. Don't fool yourself and waste precious time with half-assed desires. Acknowledge where you are and what you want, and then raise your desire to the appropriate heights. The bigger the dream, the hotter your desire must burn.

LAW 3

Faith Conquers Fear: Respect Faith's Ability to Keep You Standing and Fear's Ability to Bring You Down

You have to have faith. There are ups and downs in this business—nothing's absolute. One year's different from the next. That's just how music is. —DJ Khalil

There was many a time where, you know, we'd go and have enough money to get there and know that while we were there, we'd have to … sell a beat to go home or there was no going home. —Dow, Tha Bizness

OBSERVATION

We love this craft. There's something about the creative expression of music that's hard-wired into our DNA, our very souls. Our hearts beat like the groove of an 808 and a kick drum. The cells flowing through the blood in our veins are shaped like whole notes. The force that beckons us to make music is the same magnetic, instinctual mechanism that directs birds to head south when it gets chilly. It's the same natural impulse that wondrously guides sharks and turtles thousands of miles to their birthplaces to find mates.

It's built into our coding, and eventually, it finds you if you've been chosen. Like I said previously, I ignored the impulse to make beats as a freshman in college, but by senior year, I'd been completely captivated and dominated by beatmaking. And it wasn't long before I was introduced to a producer's faith and fear.

REALIZATION

While visiting the Shady Records office in New York City some years ago, I met a producer and we ended up having a dope chat. This producer, who later sent me some beats that I thought were pretty good, was another cat who'd been making beats for ten-plus years and was still waiting for that elusive break. He told me stories of the frustration involved in being denied production success, the years upon years of heartbreak in not yet being able to obtain his goals. He mentioned personal problems that chipped away at his focus, faith, and persistence. And he said that he had to step away for a break every so often because the chase overwhelmed him. He was a true example of the grinding mortar-and-pestle nature of production and of how absolutely important it is that you *maintain amazing faith* if you want to be a successful, well-respected producer.

We risk venturing into a dangerous place when we love something so intensely. Anything you love with a passion has the potential to inflict unbearable misery; deep love and pain go hand in hand. Music production follows this abiding principle. In the past, you had to love production with all your soul, but thanks to the baby boom of producers in recent years, combined with the decline in traditional work, you have to love it even more now. I've seen quite a few producers broken by the chase, angry with the world because they haven't achieved their goals. The disappointment colors their faces and infects their demeanors. They float through industry events and beat battles, drifting through the crowd like discouraged ghosts, walking shells of their formerly enthused, beatmaking selves.

Faith

How do you avoid becoming one of these ghosts? How do we balance our love for this craft with the frustration involved in courting success? *You must develop and maintain enough faith to continue the pursuit of production until it's your time.* "Faith plays a huge part in sustaining yourself in *this* business and [in] achieving any kind of success," DJ Khalil told me. You'll have to learn that your love for creation and your faith in the manifestation of your dream must be enough to sustain you as you give it your all, year after year.

After occupying my position at Dynamic Producer and being in constant contact with successful producers, I realized that I never had enough faith to sustain myself in the business. But the great producers that my colleagues and I looked up to were those who possessed unyielding faith. They believed in their life's mission, they had faith that their track would make the album, they had faith that their royalty check was in the mail, and they had faith that signing a deal would benefit them. They were willing to walk blindfolded off a cliff and pray that they landed in a soft place. Without that kind of faith, they wouldn't be where they are.

Do you want to learn the secrets of successful producers? You're reading one of them now. It's no accident that amazingly gifted and successful people have accomplished what they have. *They have basic principles operating inside of them at maximum levels:* "...believing in God, having faith, and just knowing that stuff is going to happen, even when it doesn't look like it," said Hen of Tha Bizness. You've got to be built to believe and hold on. If that's not who you are as a person, you're going to have a difficult time getting through this business.

What if your daughter gets sick before your quarterly publishing statement arrives, and you don't have money to pay the hospital? What if there's a dispute on the splits, and the money gets held up, and now you don't have the money to pay for your wedding? This is real life. If you want a career as a producer, then these possibilities are in your future. Make sure you're employing faith as you keep moving forward—faith that is built upon as much informa- tion as possible so you can make educated decisions. And when you can't gather more information, and things are out of your hands, that's when you have to take your faith to the next level.

Fear

It seems logical that if we discuss the power of faith as an aspiring producer, we must also discuss its evil opposite, fear. You'll see fear discussed many times in this book. To me, fear is the greatest destroyer of hu- man potential. Of all the emotions, fear apathetically rolls the most bodies of dead dreams into freshly dug graves. It deserves every bit of attention I will give it in this book. Although I don't think I was ever really racked with uncontrollable fear as I was producing, I know it was in my heart, beneath the surface, caus- ing damage, ripping up my potential, freezing me stiff when I was supposed to be moving and execut- ing. I've had to learn to acknowledge it, tussle with it, and overcome it, and it's still a major hurdle in creativity and business. I know it's possible that fear is doing the same thing to some of you. Of fear, Troy Taylor says,

> Fear is not a word that I use often … because I'm a Jesus Christ believer. If I even think that I'm

being afraid of something, I just start to pray and allow God to remove the fear. *I'm not afraid to lose and start all over again.* If that looks like it's gonna happen, *I've already accepted it....* I'm just already prepared. So fear is gone.

Troy has been through it all. He's seen enough music-business hell to appreciate his successes and accomplishments. Here's a man who's suffered challenging business and personal situations: the dissolution of a decade-long production-business partnership, the IRS with its boot on his neck, payments for financial mistakes that someone else made, a divorce, and time he missed spending with his son because he worked so hard. Through all of this, he never let fear paralyze him or stop him. When you have enough faith to keep moving forward and never fear sinking to the bottom, you give yourself the kind of strength you need to keep pushing ahead in a business such as this.

I had some in-depth conversations with Tha Bizness about how they've managed to keep fear at bay. When I asked the production duo about their experiences with fear, Hen said,

Definitely, we've gone through a lot of ups and downs, trying to figure out how to be successful, how to be good, and fear always comes with that. And [with] the type of lifestyle [we lead], the type of music that we're making, and even the types of decisions that we make, there's a lot of fear.

Sometimes we're stepping out of the box [and] we're not playing it safe.

After exploring the history of these two cats, I know they've seen more than their fair share of challenges that make those words ring with truth. Their studio was broken into and they were robbed of all their tracks and every piece of equipment that could fit through the door. In the blink of an eye, thousands of dollars' worth of studio equipment and millions of dollars' worth of potential intellectual property vanished. In addition to disappointment, anger, and distrust, fear was there, waiting to set in. Questions such as "Are we going be able to re-create what we did?" "How are we going to come back from this?" and "What does this mean to our careers?" flooded their minds. Hen explains:

> You look at fear setting in; you look at a lot of these things that come about when stuff like that happens to you. It rips your whole career apart, and for us, it just makes us stronger. We were able to adapt to new software, we were able to adapt to new circumstances, new situations, and understand that you can't take away the skill. Even when we understood who did it, we could tell them [we] appreciated it, [because] it took us to a whole different level.

Instead of letting negative emotions and thought patterns derail them, Hen and Dow chose to place their faith in moving forward and to see the blessing

in disguise. Being stripped bare revealed to them that
they couldn't be robbed of the talents God gave them
or the skills they'd spent years perfecting. It took
the worst of situations to reveal their true strength,
which is how life enjoys reminding us of who we are
and what we're capable of.

This production duo perfectly embodies the mindset I've seen time and time again from successful producers. Says Dow, "You can't be afraid to go to zero.
Most people don't succeed, because they're scared
of an idea. They're scared of something that's not
even real." He continued by discussing some fearful
thought processes that I myself have seen producers
confront:

> "Damn, I don't want to go on this trip to this
> conference where I may meet people to help me out
> because I'm scared of not having [the] money to
> pay [for] the car next month." You just gotta get
> off your ass and go and figure out a way to make
> it happen instead of always being scared all the
> time. The people that succeed are the people that
> believe. That's all it is; everybody else just gives up,
> [or they] just don't try. That's why they don't win.

These concepts seem simple enough, right? But
there's a difference between reading it, understanding it, and living it. Fear lurks in the hearts of the
successful just like it does in everyone else, but faith
and desire are stronger. A belief in things unseen and
unknown is one of your greatest allies when conquer-

ing fear during your pursuit of production success. Learning to put fear in its proper place is essential.

When I asked Focus whether he encountered any fear as a producer, he said,

> Every day. Every day of every week of every month of every year. Yes. I'm a family man first ... and the biggest thing for me has been providing, being a provider for my family. When the climate of music changed, and me being from the old school, me being from the sound and the genre of music I was from, it was very hard for me for the past couple of years just to fit in with these newer producers and [the] newer sound of hip-hop.

> It does get scary. You wonder where the money's gonna come from, if there's gonna be any money, if you're ever gonna have relevance again, if you're gonna be able to resurface, if you're gonna matter. There's always that fear that looms over every producer, and if anybody ever tells you otherwise, they're lying. Then that means that he's not really a producer.

> We come from a creative place in our souls that makes us emotional. A lot of people are good with masking it, but there's a point in their day or in their month or week or whatever where they'll go someplace and have that vulnerable moment. And it's what makes us who we are, and it's part of what keeps us driven.

> So, there's not a producer that I know that hasn't ever feared ... being obsolete, or being irrelevant, or being in a place where they wouldn't be able to pick themselves up and start over or reinvent. There's always a fear or insecurity.

Jesus. I'm not even sure I know what to say to that, other than that he's absolutely right. If you are blessed enough to get a career moving, to do this full time and take care of your kids, you'll benefit from having this quote swimming through the back of your mind. It'll make you employ everything you learn in this book to make sure you're creating to the best of your ability, you're managing yourself to the best of your ability, and you're watching your business to the best of your ability. Do whatever you must to keep those fears at bay. Because they will come. But you had a warning, so you'll be prepared, and you'll already be doing what's necessary to keep the ball rolling. Use the fear. Let what you've read be a motivational tool. As Chuck Greene says,

> Fear is needed in order to be successful. If you don't have fear, you're so confident that you don't see that there's an opportunity to f*ck it up. You can control the fear and make the fear create positive energy toward completing the task or getting something done. Fear is needed; use it to your advantage. When you meet a powerful exec, and he sits you down and wants to talk about your music, you *should* have *some* fear.

Use the fear of not succeeding and the fear of not being the best; use those fears to your advantage, to make yourself do what you must, to achieve what you set out to achieve.

And when you've achieved your goals, then what? You're home free, right? Wrong. Once you find success, a different kind of fear sets in, a brand of fear that I didn't get far enough to experience but that some of you who'll rise through the ranks may. Says REO of the Soundkillers,

I don't believe I fully understood the idea of fear being a factor in my career until I actually had one to lose. Becoming [a producer], I wasn't scared because I really truly loved it, and [there] was a lot of innocence left in me. I was literally making music from a place that had nothing to do with monetary gain or anything; it was just like "I love doing this," so I just did it. And then one of the greatest and scariest things happened to me when I got my first placement. My passion became my job. It's like they say, "You are only as good as your last hit" and sometimes they're right. Whatever you hit with, whatever is your biggest placement, the timer starts ticking as soon as that happens, and it's like a graph. You have this high point, and then it goes down, and it just keeps falling until you get another [placement].

Usually people tend to remember you by what you have accomplished, not by what you are going to accomplish. I knew this was my first huge accomplishment, and I needed to make sure that it wasn't my only one. Time goes by and you watch your song go down the charts until it's no longer there. Now what? The fear of never getting another placement or being "that person who did that one thing a while back" is strong and can overwhelm you

> if you let it. Stay strong mentally and spiritually, always do your best, create from a real place that takes you back to when you did it only for the love, and I believe you will always have success.

REO's situation is unique, and I'm glad that I'm able to include his experience in this book. He started out with a placement with the diva herself, Beyoncé. Coming out of the gate, he set a very high standard for himself, and he faced the challenge of trying to land placements that were equally substantial and relevant:

> You know, I was on Beyoncé's album, [which] luckily did so well; she had ten Grammy nominations, and she released two Thanksgiving specials and DVDs that went Platinum. I don't think [any] other album has had that kind of longevity in a while.

> That album carried for years, and when she came out with her new album, I [could have] been that guy—"Oh, I did that track on Beyoncé," "Oh, which one did you do?" "Nah, it's on her old album." It's like the worst feeling, like you want to stay relevant, you want to stay on top, and that fear of just the time running out, and you know you need to make something happen so that people don't forget about you.

The fear of success is a tricky bastard; he hides in the alleys of your mind, waiting for your imagination to paint pleasant pictures of "what if." Then, he springs from the shadows to kill positivity with thoughts of being unable to maintain success, being revealed as a no-talent hack, or crumbling under the heavy weight of future responsibilities. While you're examining your fears, watch not only for the fear of failure but for his more obscure cousin, too.

Break Beats

One of the most important things you can do to keep your faith healthy is to take creative production breaks. I spoke earlier about how grinding toward becoming a producer can be a process that breaks down your body, grates on your mind, and wrings the juice out of your soul. The frustration of pursuit will eat away at some of you, and you will need a break. Others may advise that you have to go hard every day, put your feelings aside, and keep it moving. But I've been there, and I've experienced this. I had to take a few breaks to handle the mental drainage, and I hadn't been making music nearly as long as some of the producers I've come across in my travels.

I think it's crucial that you step back and give yourself a chance to clear your mind, make sure you're making the right moves, and recommit to the grind. Use this time to gain a fresh take on making music, and in return, you will approach the creative process with a new frame of mind. Review and reaffirm your vision; remember why you're here. Come to terms with the fact that you don't know how long this journey will take, but you do know that you're going to give everything you have. Remind yourself that you do this because you love it, and you'll be doing it forever, regardless of the checks. I know you damn sure want a fat check, but remind yourself that being blessed to create is already a delicious cake. The check is simply the tasty icing.

Take some time from actually producing and immerse yourself in different styles of music. Absorb some classics and figure out what made them such. Study what's popular. Even when you're not making beats, *you still need to be doing something creative daily*.

Even people who do what they love take vacations. But don't go for too long. There's a producer every day who stops for a short break and ends up never going back. A week turns into two, and two weeks turn into a month. Next thing you know, the keyboard is napping peacefully beneath a thick blanket of dust.

THE FINAL MIX

I hope I've given you an accurate portrayal of the importance of both faith and fear in production. Although you're not likely to hear your favorite producers sit on a panel and discuss these personal concepts at a conference, they deal with these issues on a daily basis. It's a part of being a creative person and a part of our business. A major reason that successful producers are in the position they're in is that they've developed the ability to master faith and fear.

Some of us may never make it to the big leagues, but we don't all have to be superstars to live well and make good music. Regardless, you won't know unless you program certain emotions and thought patterns into your mind and refuse to abandon them. You must live daily with a beautiful mix of mental strength, faith, and endurance. Above all, you must be committed to improving, *because the journey is easier to travel if your skills are up to par*. That's the real key.

When your skill level reaches undeniability and elicits the consistent screwface (an honor bestowed upon the hottest of tracks; it's essentially your listeners scrunching up their faces as if they smelled something horrible because the music is so funky), you've added a new dimension to your courtship with production.

"One day you're down and out, and the next day you get a call from somebody, and it completely changes your whole perspective," says DJ Khalil. Hold on as long as you can. *If your skills are where they should be*, then maybe it'll be you receiving that life-changing call. But in the meantime, build and maintain your faith and bust your ass to be as incredible as you can be. Avoid my naïveté: *Never underestimate the power of faith to propel you forward and of fear to hold you back*.

Part 2: What Can Stop Me?

LAW 4

The Great Wall: Become Emotionally Separate from Criticism

I expect so much from my music. You want people to like it right away, [but] it doesn't always work that way. —DJ Khalil

To take offense to something is a sign of weakness to me; that's the beginning of the breakdown of them getting what they want because you [got] angry. —Troy Taylor

OBSERVATION

The critiquing process is like weightlifting. If you're familiar with the science of the sport, you know that when you lift weights, you break down your muscles through the process of performing multiple reps to the point of fatigue. When you rest, the muscle fibers repair themselves, becoming stronger in the process. Over time, through continuous muscle destruction and construction, you become "swole."

This is the exact same route we need to take as producers. You must *let people listen to your music. And not your people—random people! You must give your music out and ask for opinions.* The critiques you receive will be the destructive repetitions for your production muscles, and as you apply the critiques to your new tracks, your creative muscles will be rebuilt stronger, forcing improvement. But if you're scared to be critiqued, how will you ever benefit from this process? It's absolutely essential that you're able to positively use negative responses to improve your music. You will have to learn to be emotionally separate from the judgment of your music so you can grow.

Double Elimination

I was at a beat battle in Atlanta many years ago. Two gentlemen gracefully moseyed onto the stage, each with the expectation of leaving his opponent battered with his most bananas beats and advancing to the next round with ease. I watched each producer hand off his beat CDs to the DJ and call out his weapon of choice—"Gimme number five" and "Let's run with seven." Our host for the evening, the legendary Fort Knox, called the match and the beats began. And they were trash. They were a heaping, steaming pile of rubbish. Although the crowd sat in awkward silence, I could see the imaginary tomatoes and turnips being hurled toward the stage. As a result of the disaster coming from the speakers, the judges decided to pull the double-elimination card, only after each judge took his turn meticulously dismantling and destroying the beats. Then both beatmakers were cast shamelessly from the ballot.

Now here's where it got interesting. One of the two moseyed off the stage, ungracefully this time, and went back to bury himself in his corner of the club. The other burst into an inferno of anger, yelling, "That's bullshit!" and channeling all his anger into a verbal assault on the judges. Then he raged on for a good few minutes while the host tried to weather the storm by reminding the young man that these were just the rules of the competition and he didn't need to respond in that manner.

We all have a decision to make in moments like this, and I hope that after you read this book, some of you, if you didn't have it before, will have the emotional intelligence needed to make the right decision.

You know what both producers should have done? Both of them should have grabbed the mic, turned around, and said, "Thanks for listening to and judging my tracks. I know you weren't feeling my music, necessarily, but do you have any suggestions on how I can improve?" That's the emotionally intelligent move. That angry producer should have said, "I'm passionate about this art and business, and I'd like to know if I can keep in contact with you so that when I improve, I'll have some product for you. Also, maybe you can continue to share some wisdom and knowledge as I progress."

That's what a person who's serious about his craft would have done. Easier said than done, yes I know this, but ideally, that serious producer would have recognized the fact that his art was not him, that the judges weren't critiquing him as a man but were critiquing his music. And that's what he came onstage to do: be critiqued. Furthermore, that same person would have realized that he's here in this environment playing his music *for other people.* The judges and the crowd were there to give him an opinion, to express how they felt about what they heard. The self-aware producer would have looked around and thought to himself that he has an audience and a panel of music professionals at his disposal to give him constructive criticism. People pay good money for that opportunity nowadays, so take advantage of it when you get a chance.

I understand the mindset of the cat who got angry. It's easy to let that emotion manhandle you and cloud your judgment. It's harder to keep your cool and figure out how to use the pain to evolve. But you producers are in a hard line of work. You've got to know when to put your emotions to the side and use logic. You must be able to ask yourself: "How can I benefit from this situation? How can I benefit from what seems to be a tragic disappointment at the moment? I'm embarrassed, I'm angry, but how can I make this serve me?" If someone isn't feeling your music, simply ask about it. Perhaps what they offer will be a gem of wisdom and perhaps it won't, but you won't know until *you put your fear aside* and *have the courage to ask.*

REALIZATION

Do not make beats like me. I dodged critiques like they were blasting hot from the tip of a double-barrel shotgun. I was terrified and subsequently hated being judged. I thought I was slick, so I played only my best tracks for people to listen to. I invited criticism *on my own terms* or when I shaped the situation to get the best response. Were you a hip-hop lover from the east coast? Oh, well then, you were a perfect candidate to hear my beats! I'd fire up the production immediately because I knew I had a better chance of your digging my music. I couldn't bear discovering that I wasn't as good as I thought. I had a horrible habit of identifying with my music: I became my beats to the point where if someone said my music was trash, I believed I was trash. I carried the disappointment willingly, letting it fester inside of my ego like an old, rotting sore. That's what made the critiquing process so painful; I hadn't learned how to separate myself from my art. We were one being.

As you listen to the critiques of people who are in a position to help you ascend, you must learn to walk the line of being passionate about your music without identifying with it so much that you take things so personally. You are not your beats, my friend. It's a piece of music. You'll have to learn to have thicker skin if you're going to be a producer, because you'll *never* please everybody.

If you sit on your music and disregard the potential growth that comes from getting opinions, you waste precious time—not a resource to waste in your line of work. You can't afford to do that kind of disservice to your own progression. When speaking about negative critiques, DJ Khalil said, "[They make] me work harder; there [are] a lot of times when I don't feel like I'm good enough." Ultimately, DJ Khalil uses the critiquing process to fuel the desire to work even harder. And you should be doing the same thing. Let them tear your music apart so you can build your sound back up. Don't let those beats sit on that hard drive unheard! (And also keep in mind that the guy with multiple placements on your favorite artist's album says he doesn't think he's good enough. That's why he works relentlessly. *Yes, you're competing with professionals who have that kind of mindset. Heavy!*)

Focus reinforces the importance of being able to seek and accept criticism in one's career: "I don't think there's ever a point in your career where you don't need critiques. Did I take it well? Not when I first got started. That just taught me how to become humble." Focus learned to appreciate criticism's role in production and eventually put his ego aside so he could absorb the wisdom that came from those critiques. Also, he stressed the need for balance in accepting critiques: "You definitely have to be humble, you have to accept constructive criticism, but everybody has an opinion at the same time, so ... do you want to hear everybody's opinion? No."

There's another way to examine this situation. Since I switched from the creative to the business end, the dark side, I've learned from the professionals in my circle that there are different ways of looking at your tracks, these pieces of yourself. Remember that if you're working in a commercial capacity—that is, you're trying to sell a piece of art—then once it's finished, technically speaking, it's not for you. Its purpose is to become a part of someone else's artistic vision. After that, it's supposed to be enjoyed commercially and take music-loving consumers at the end of the creative pipeline where *they* need to go. That's the point of selling music, right? Then don't obsess over it like it's never supposed to leave the hard drive.

I love Troy's perspective on this, which helped me see the error of my own ways when I was younger. He says, "If I'm making music, and I'm being of service to the people, it ain't necessarily for me, so if it's not necessarily for me, how can I tell you what you want for yourself?" All the more reason to keep it cool and use those lukewarm responses as tinder to ignite your creative fire. Furthermore, he explained to me that he understood the value of what he was producing and knew that he was turning out music that, even though it may not have resonated with that particular listener, was still up to his professional standards. Troy's insight into his own skill level gives him the ability to let people make their comments as they see fit, but if those comments are negative, it doesn't affect him negatively. That's an emotional barricade you can build for yourself once your product reaches a level of professional consistency.

I know there are thousands of you holding on to those tracks for dear life, scared to let them go. Push that baby bird out of the nest! There are people close to me who've begun making beats, and I never get a track. They know of my expertise, and they don't bother to get my opinion. To them, I'm a homicidal butcher, standing there revving a glistening, five-foot chainsaw, wearing a leather smock bloodied with the juicy bits of other producers' beats. On my face I wear an evil grin so wide I could eat a banana sideways. And instead of seeing an opportunity to grow, these novice producers envision the splattered blood, guts, and musical limbs of their precious productions scattered about the room. But I understand; I saw critiques the same way. And if I avoided critiques, and producers I know are avoiding them, I know some of you are, too! As hard as it is to figure out what you're doing, especially when you're just starting, Lord knows you need that direction.

The way to build your strength when receiving negative critiques is to simply receive them. Walk toward the butcher. The first critiques hit like a heavyweight punch to the gut. You curl up; the shot sends you reeling to the floor. But you get back up. And you keep taking those shots. Over time, you're taking body shots like a champ. And that's when you start objectively plucking the juicy fruits of improvement from the tree of criticism without the pain.

THE FINAL MIX

When you ascend to the point where you're getting placements left and right, then critiques become a little less relevant (not irrelevant!). At that point, charts, dance floors, streams, checks, and your successful peers are your critics.

If you're still hustling tracks and have yet to attain some success, then there's room to grow. But here's the thing about becoming a master—there's always room to grow. Passion and drive inspire endless improvement. Put your ego aside and let your listeners rip up those beats. Remember that getting offended, angry, or upset shouldn't be an option. Use the temporary defeat to work toward a victory.

Hen of Tha Bizness says,

> For me, [critiques are] always appreciated. You hate
> to hear when somebody doesn't like something, but
> you love to see the scrunch face. So it just goes hand

in hand; if they're not loving that, then what can we do to make them love it?

Immediately, the disappointment shifts to figuring out what they can do to get the reaction they want—how can we get better? The emotion fuels the desire to work toward excellence. Emulate those who've achieved what you're trying to achieve! Use the negative to fuel the positive!

Side Note: The Cabinet

I would absolutely recommend having a "music cabinet" (you know, like the president's cabinet members)—a mixture of music lovers, fellow producers, and regular people who can be honest with you and tell you what they think. This is a huge advantage you should give yourself and something that I learned to do years into producing. Every few weeks or so, a package of music goes out, and you trust your group to listen and give you the honest, constructive feedback you need. Make this happen; it's essential for growth.

> When I started going to people's offices and they were like, "You know, dog, don't quit your day job," I was like, "Word? You don't know what the hell you're talking about!" And you can't talk to people like that. And I look back now, and I'm glad that I did not come out when I thought I was the hotness, 'cuz I wasn't. —Focus

LAW 5

Silence the Snob: Ride, but Never on a High Horse

OBSERVATION

As producers, should we ever put our standards to the side? Can our standards be so high that sometimes they end up hurting us? I came up during the time when an artist had to be a lyrical beast. As much as I loved the beat, I insisted on listening only to artists with excellent lyrical ability. When I became old enough to comprehend poetic depth, it was '95 or '96, around the time when Jay-Z dropped *Reasonable Doubt*. I remember immersing myself in the complexities of the first two verses of "Feelin' It" that I recorded off of Hot 97. I was so deep into those first two verses that I didn't even know there was a third verse until I copped a tape of the album. What I didn't realize at the time was that by growing up in the lyrical East Coast nexus of artists like Jay-Z, Nas, GZA, and Biggie, I was habituating myself to a high standard of lyricism. Now that's not a bad thing at all, but it caused me to over-look opportunities years later.

When I was in the full swing of production, I would come across artists who showed interest in my music, yet I foolishly chose not to work with them. To me, if you weren't capable of spitting Nas-like heat, then you were trash. There was a massive disconnect between what I grew up listening to (East Coast, lyrical MCs) and what was growing popular in Atlanta. So, when I had the opportunity to get into the studio or get some beats to Joe Blow Rapper Guy, I wouldn't touch it because Joe Blow from the east side of Atlanta didn't fit my perception of what kind of witty, lyrical MC should grace my instrumentals.

REALIZATION

I was a music snob. I was so quick to look down on artists who weren't lyrically deep and complex, brimming with colorful metaphors, vivid stories, and intricate poetical mechanics. At that point in my production career, I thought I was surrounded by rolling hills of Southern musical trash.

Now, in hindsight, I know that attitude caused me to make poor decisions. The positives of working with anyone interested in my music—studio experience, the opportunity to build my brand, and a placement on *something*—would have far outweighed the initial discomfort of what I assumed would be associating with garbage.

In addition, I wasn't even actively seeking out cats I thought would be worthy of my tracks. Not every rapper was down with that crunk, snappy-finger, soulless trash during the mid-2000s. There were a lot of quality MCs running around Atlanta, but I wasn't seeking them out. So not only did the music snob inside of me cause me to ignore interested artists, I didn't even put real effort into searching for and working with MCs whose art I did respect and admire. I killed myself on both sides.

There's a twofold approach to looking at this mistake. First, from an economic point of view, this is art and business; we have wants and we have needs. I had a full-time gig and minimal expenses, so sitting on my high horse couldn't hurt me financially. Some of you who've taken the plunge and quit your jobs won't have the advantage of being in that position. In that case, you're going to let Joe Blow Rapper Guy throw you some bread and then you'll give him whatever he wants.

The second way we have to look at this is from the point of view of the career. Paying projects aren't falling out of the sky. It's grown increasingly difficult to succeed: you have to work with as many people as you can to build a brand. You don't have the luxury to miss any opportunities because *you never know what can happen with a song*. Artists whose CDs I would have chucked out of my car window ended up dominating the charts years later. Anything and anybody has the potential to be a hit or a stepping stone—just listen to the radio. For a producer, the artist is secondary: potential clients will really just want to know if you've got more tracks like the one that blew up.

As well, you have to factor in your reputation in the game. Warns Fuego, "Don't ever back away from an opportunity because you personally don't like the artist or his music, for whatever reason. That's unprofessional, and you can't afford to be looked at that way." With that said, how do we strike the balance between our standards of quality and what's necessary for our careers? I'm not suggesting that you turn every artist away or collaborate with every artist, but whatever you do, be conscious of your decisions. Maybe you need a check. Maybe your brand is more important than cash. Maybe you have to put aside what you want and focus on what you need. Whatever you decide, don't make beats like me and impetuously assume that opportunities to collaborate are beneath you. Those opportunities can be important milestones in your career. Having a few records under my belt could have been rocket fuel for my mission, forcing me to improve more quickly and expand my brand. Sadly, I'll never know.

When I asked the pros about this situation, each one had very interesting opinions that weren't far off from what I've advised. When you're at that level, everything is a factor—the money, the reputation, and the potential. At that point, music is both your art and the way you've been making a living and handling your responsibilities—your significant other, your kids, and the mortgage.

When you're dealing with artists who don't meet your creative standards but have a check for a track, Needlz advises, "You sell it; [not selling is] not an option. Most times, you can take that money and do some good for your family. You never know what a song could do." These words are absolutely true.

From more of a creative point of view, DJ Khalil said that he would try it out and see if he could bring that artist into his world, that he would try to do something new with the artist or make something that he would want to hear him on. I thought that was an incredible way to look at the situation. He continued, "Maybe I can bring something out of him that he didn't know was there." *This* is what a producer is. *This* is what a producer does. Instead of behaving like me—folding my arms and turning up my nose like a child—a producer looks for an opportunity to shape an artist with *his* music. A real producer tries to mold the situation and put that artist in a new creative space. Who knows what's possible then?

THE FINAL MIX

If I'd had the perspective I have now, I would have done something like Khalil suggested and brought those artists into my creative world. It's always an interesting experience hearing an artist on a track you didn't expect. In today's market, it's critical that you pay close attention to *every* opportunity and make sure you maximize everything that comes your way. If you're going to pass something up, be sure! Don't be like me and let your ego do the thinking for you.

One last point. The elitist-producer point of view goes beyond just working with certain artists—the music snob within can keep you confined to a genre as well. If you are talented enough to create music in multiple genres, watch out for the small, nagging voice within that says, "I only make this. This other genre, that's not cool, so we don't mess with that." Try to follow your creativity wherever it takes you, regardless of genre or artist. Seek as many opportunities as possible to make an artist sound amazing on your production, whatever that production may be. This should always be your goal.

LAW 6
Iron, Man: Develop the Strength Necessary for Success

Now, this won't be easy—I'm going to get clowned for this. But this isn't about me, so I'm going to bite the bullet and spit it out so you can win. As I look back at myself as an aspiring producer, I realize that I was a soft, six-foot-three-inch human Snuggle Bear. I was overly sensitive. I was emotional. I had skin about as thick as a sheet of tissue paper. I was easily angered by trivial slights and situations. I was scared of rejection and hated being critiqued. If you offended my business, my music, or me as a man, I took it personally, clouding my judgment as a result.

REALIZATION

Some of the most important things I've learned on the path to self-discovery are about the development of mental fortitude, the ability to adequately handle the challenges of your environment, the freedom associated with *not taking things too personally*, and the gift of *recovering from your initial anger*. These concepts are integral to maintaining composure and happiness not only as a person, but especially as a businessman who sells a product he personally creates. It's difficult to survive in the entertainment business while being too sensitive. You'll waste time being angry and upset, dwelling on being offended instead of focusing on the craft.

As you aspire to produce, you'll be beaten, battered, and bruised. People will disrespect you—at events, instead of looking at you, they'll focus their eyes on every other person in the room and check their phones while you try to pitch your music. They'll snort deeply and hock a thick, giant loogie all over your creativity. They'll call you out in the middle of a crowded producer showcase and yell, "You ain't got it, homie. Give it up! Why don't you take up crocheting instead? You'll probably make blankets better than you make beats!" People *will* attempt to hustle you—they'll send you contracts that propose to rob you and relegate you to the status of a slave as they pimp your music. They'll reject you, giving you the thumbs-down to music that is absolutely hot, because for them, it's more fun to be a jerk.

Once you let these situations hurt and upset you, and you can't let them go, you lose your power. Try to *give no one the power to derail your train.* And notice I said *try*, because as I've learned, this is a difficult concept to live your life by. Personally, if I'm going to stop or slow down, it will be through my own decision or fault. *You* will not stop me. I control what goes on in my mind, nobody else. You've got to adopt that resilient way of thinking and feeling because, quite often, you'll be tried in the entertainment business. An easily bruised ego, a nasty temper, or fragile feelings—these are all dangerous to anyone who wants to succeed in the entertainment industry. If you suffer from these traits, stop now and commit to strapping on the armor necessary to fight through the negative circumstances you will face in the business.

The production game is like anything else in life where there isn't a spot for everybody. A giant, angry gardener comes along to weed out those who aren't strong enough. Yes, you've got to have good music. Yes, you've got to network. And of course, you've got to be aware of the business, but *you must be mentally tough and thick-skinned*. I lived on the other side and you see where it got me—nowhere.

When I told Focus that because I was both emotional and naïve, I wasted a lot of time and energy being upset over things I wouldn't even acknowledge today, to my surprise he revealed that he's dealt with the same issues.

> I was an emotional kid, a super-emotional kid, so it was definitely a development. I used to get taken advantage of a lot because I come from a house of big love and big hearts, and I tried to go into the industry and be like "I'm not gonna be like

everyone else, I'm gonna do it with integrity, and people are gonna gravitate to me, because I am the way I am," and they ran through me. You do get to a point where you wake up and you say, "I'm not gonna let this happen anymore."

You can either start strengthening yourself now or gain your strength by having the industry hammer on you until you toughen. I propose that you be proactive about it, but either way, becoming strong is a necessity to get where you're going. If you've got a little Snuggle Bear within, learn to separate yourself into two different people when it's time to go to work. Those parts of you that don't mesh well with the business of selling music, leave those at home when working in the lion's den. I asked master relationship-builder and super-connector Dow of Tha Bizness if there are any parts of his and Hen's personalities that don't mesh well with the business of hustling music, and he gave me the dopest response:

> It may be all of our personality, but you'll never know that. That's what we'll take with us, what we'll talk [about] amongst ourselves. That's the greatest game, never knowing what's really what.

Hen chimed in with, "and understanding that *perception* is key…. The *perception* you're gonna get is that *we were made for this, we were bred for this.*" If these cats have certain emotions running through their hearts, you'll never know. They've learned to compartmentalize themselves by developing business personas, and they're strong enough to keep their emotions tucked away while they're focused on handling business.

Taking the Loss

Once we understand that we can't get too emotional and negatively react to every offense, how do we handle ourselves in the lion's den? How do we conduct ourselves when we've got unscrupulous managers, A&Rs, and artists trying to hustle us? Understand that some of you *will* be taking some losses and punishment when you're new. Unfortunately, when you're unknown, you don't have as much leverage and power. It's simply part of the game, so don't blow a gasket; keep your head up and keep looking forward. Beat-hustler extraordinaire and former Dynamic Producer member Fuego advises,

> Don't get emotional—the music business is very competitive, and most of the participants are out for their best interests. You win some; you lose some. Sometimes you'll just have to take the loss. However, karma always comes back to [those] who do other people dirty, so be fair in everything you do.

Fuego makes a good point, and I want to supplement his quote with something shared by Focus:

> You just gotta learn when to speak and when not to speak, and sometimes you might not be able to speak

at all. It's one of those things where you go home and you look at your kids or you look at your wife or if it's not that, look at the fact that you're living someplace, look at the fact that you might have a car payment or that you need money in your bank account, and you look at the necessities and you … go in and do what you have to do. There are a lot of people that get up for a nine-to-five and hate their boss, but they go and they slave for their nine-to-five because they have no choice. And this is our nine-to-five, so you get up and you do what you gotta do.

When it's your time to do what you have to, do it, instead of getting frustrated and reacting.

While I'm all about reeling in your emotions when you have to take a loss, there will come times when you'll be flat-out disrespected. In those situations, you'll have to do your best to set some professional standards so that nonsense doesn't keep occurring. When you believe you're not being treated as you should, stand up and make the situation known. I know it can feel like someone is doing you a favor by showing interest or purchasing one of your tracks— you feel like you have to make this opportunity work so you can get your career moving—and that breeds a tendency to keep your mouth shut and take people's crap. Remember, they want what you have and you want what they have; it's a business transaction. Avoid, as much as possible, acting meek and mousy, or that's the way you'll be treated. Reputations spread, and they are king in this industry.

Troy gave me some invaluable information that not only demonstrates how to fix a situation when you're not being treated fairly, but also touches upon being paid according to your rate, dealing with budget cuts, and keeping people to their word:

> Now there is a thing where you can be offended by someone treating you less than your worth. When you know how much you're worth, and you know that they're not treating you at the level of your worth, you have an obligation to let them know. "No, I can do more than that," or "No, I do this; I don't just do that," or "Well, you know, you're not paying me according to the job that I can do, so please explain to me why I'm getting this low [fee]." "Well, the budget." "I know, you're gonna say the budget's low."

> That's the thing that people love to say; the first thing that they love to say is "The budget's low, we don't have enough." "Well, can we agree that if we do more than just one, it can be this price, but if it's one, it's this price? If I do it for this price right now, I don't want it to go into your system as this being my rate."

> So there are things that you have to make sure you let them know. Nowadays, you have to do it in an e-mail. Because [people] forget. They really push the selective-memory button, and if you don't have it in an e-mail, then it doesn't exist.

It doesn't get more specific and more real than that. You have to know when to keep silent, when to take the loss, and when to stand up for yourself, but regardless, try not to react with your negative emotions. Advises Hen of Tha Bizness,

> You must always adapt to your surroundings, to do what you do better. You have to adapt to your circumstances to be able to do what you do; that's [with] anything that you get into, any lifestyle that you become a part of.

Adapting to the environment of the music industry means evolving into a character of strength and acclimating to the frequent shots fired by the entertainment industry during the normal course of business. I'm not suggesting that you aspire to become a stiff, emotionless machine, moved by no situation, bad or good. But the stronger you become, the better you'll be able to weather the inevitable emotional storms headed for your shores.

THE FINAL MIX

Don't duplicate my mistakes by letting overactive emotions arrest your potential. Never let your anger, ego, pride, or fear do the talking for you. Never let those feelings sit your rational self down while they dictate the moves. When those moments present themselves—you know, when you're sitting at an A&R's desk and he's forking loads of chow mein into his mouth, smacking his lips, taking calls, and playing on Facebook while you're trying to play your beats, and you feel the anger bubbling within your gut—maintain your cool. That isn't the time to let the anger flare, shoot a healthy "Screw you, man!" his way, and storm out of the room. Because when you blow up, he'll call you and ask you why you didn't play that hotness when you both sat down. And you'll just smile, set a meeting, and move some tracks.

It's funny, I've come to a point where I'm rarely surprised by people's malicious behavior in all sectors of business. I hate to sound like a cynic, but people will do whatever they must to protect what they've built. And that means giving you the shaft, if necessary. It's human nature. So, although I always look for the best parts of people, I always keep one eye open, ready to dodge the bull like a matador. I expect it; this *is* the music industry, and yes, it *is* a jungle. This expectation helps me maintain my cool.

LAW 7

Unreasonable Doubt: Avoid Failure From Distrusting Your Abilities

I'm just like everybody else, I have doubts. —DJ Khalil

If I'd sold myself any shorter in my production career, I'd be a damn midget. There were times when I
chose not to work with an artist who had a different
style than my own because I doubted that my tracks
would measure up. As a result, I let opportunities
spill through my fingers like sand. It's a horrible mistake to listen to the persuasive advice hissing from
our own self-doubt, but it's especially dangerous to
us creative-minded creatures. You never know what's
behind the magic door in the music industry—a door
that doubt will tell you is rigged to explode if you
open it—but you must open it and see what happens.

OBSERVATION

Doubt, that cunning crook, bested me during an
encounter with one of my favorite artists. Several
years back, I attended the album release party for
Ghostface's *Fishscale* album. Ghost is one of the

reasons I became a sample-heavy producer: I grew up on *Ironman* and *Supreme Clientele*, and that style of hard, gritty, and soulful music was written into my DNA. I was at a swanky club in Atlanta, waiting for the brother Starks to enter the space. I ended up sitting next to Ghostface in a gigantic, half-donut-shaped leather couch, snapping pictures with the cat. It couldn't be a bigger deal for me; I may as well have been sitting in the Oval Office kicking it with Obama.

Back then, I was a shy, nervous idiot when it came to networking. Through the strength of the gods, I willed myself to ask Ghost where I could send beats. He was mad cool and kind enough to write his manager's e-mail and phone number on a promo poster.

So some days go by, and I let the mind start to whisper the nonsense that even intelligent minds tend to whisper: "Psssh! Psssssh ... You don't have anything at that level of quality, son." "You're going to make a fool of yourself, son." "Don't even waste your time. Why don't you wait till you get a little bit better?" I let doubt clamp its pointy fangs into my confidence and ooze negative, self-defeating venom throughout my thoughts. Before I knew it, I had procrastinated my ass off; weeks turned to months, and months turned into my sitting here reflecting on it. What a shame.

I did this a number of times. I was constantly around people at music-video shoots who could have made a difference, but I doubted myself and held on to my material because I wasn't confident in my catalog as a whole. I may have had a few nice joints, but because I was so competitive with myself, I needed my *whole* beat CD to be crazy (a feat rarely achieved by any producer).

REALIZATION

You have to figure out where you are sonically so you don't end up underestimating your talent. Underestimated talent is the full moon that turns a cute puppy of confidence into a raging werewolf of doubt. I think your recipients should let you know if you've got what they're looking for or if you're up to par. Don't automatically write yourself off and purposely avoid opportunities because you're waiting until you transform into Timbaland. In the beginning, yes, you may need to wait a bit, but you risk the danger of always holding on to that thinking. Do you know how many tracks producers have written off as garbage until an artist heard potential and then recorded a hit record? Producers always stuff a few beats on the back of the beat CD, beats they don't really believe in, but they have to fill the gaps, and oftentimes it's those very beats that end up getting selected. Yes, you should critique yourself. Yes, you should know where you are and always strive to improve. But don't purposefully pass up opportunities because you don't believe you've got the glow yet. Send in the music, and ask your prospects what they think. Build and maintain and keep sending tracks out as you progress.

My experience gives me the impression that doubt affects more producers than I initially thought. It's a part of being human and certainly a part of being a creative person. I asked DJ Khalil if he ever doubted himself. Much to my surprise, he responded, "I doubt myself every day. I didn't make Drake's [first] album because I doubted myself. [I] didn't really feel like I measured up ... [so I] psyched myself out of it."

Talk about being speechless! It was inconceivable that a producer of *his success and talent* was plagued by an emotion that plagued me, and we were as far away from each other on the success spectrum as you could be. Needlz mentioned having doubts over a decade deep into his career. That voice of negativity, whispering vicious thoughts from some gloomy chamber in the back of our minds, can grab ahold of any of us—from those with Platinum plaques to those who wish they had one. All of a sudden, you're sitting at the computer, afraid to click "send." Try to conquer your hissing voice of doubt. The difference between success and failure lies in how quickly you address doubts the second they arrive. The longer you entertain those thoughts, the more powerful they become. When you hear them whispering to you, remember this chapter; then *shut down those doubts and grind toward an undeniable product.*

THE FINAL MIX

Some of us set such ridiculous standards for our art that we don't realize how talented we are and we impede our own progress. You know those songwriters, painters, or writers who create year after year and never think they're good enough, so they don't bother chasing after their dreams? They're flattened under the weight of their own doubts. Those lyrics never end up joining with a track, those paintings never see a gallery, and those stories never get read. You don't want to live in that self-constructed prison. Have faith in the talent the Lord blessed you with and the time you've spent working on your craft.

LAW 8:

Beats in Chains: Never Handcuff Your Tracks for Fear of Losing Them

Every artist has the potential of being big and you don't know who it's gonna be, so you give it to whoever you feel like is gonna put it out. —Troy Taylor

OBSERVATION

I hope that you are not guilty of this, but it's something I did often, and I'm positive that it hampered my production career. I would bang out decent tracks, and every once in a while I would come up with some straight heat—real dragon breath. Relishing my own genius and massaging my own ego, I would sit in my home studio, smiling like a Cheshire cat, playing the track over and over again. Eventually it came time to mix it down and place it on the beat CD. And I wouldn't. I'd handcuff the track because I was worried that some no-name artist would want to hop on my treasured work of art and waste it on an album or mixtape no one would hear, which in my mind was about as bad as having your legs broken by the mob. I wanted to be heard. I needed the news of my sonic genius to spread far and wide across the lands. I thought I couldn't afford to waste hot music on small projects. Feeling like I had to save my best work for major placements and big opportunities, I sat on my good music until I thought I was in a position to give it to an artist of *high value:* "Nah, son. Jeezy gotta have that," or "I'm holding out for Beanie on that one, baby."

You think I'm throwing exaggerated examples at you, but I actually uttered those words. Will, my roommate and business partner at the time, went to high school with Slick Pulla, one of Young Jeezy's group members and label mates during the heyday of CTE Records in Atlanta. Realizing that I had a bridge, I asked Will to pass along to Slick the track I composed so he could pass it to Jeezy. I carefully instructed Will, in slow, deliberate sentences like a mom explaining a concept beyond her toddler, to make sure Slick passed it on, that it was not for him. I didn't want Slick to get interested and lay something on my heat, throw it on a mixtape, and waste a dope beat and opportunity. It was explicitly for Jeezy!

My roommate looked at me like I had a third eye growing from the middle of my forehead. I didn't see what the problem was; things tend to make sense to you when you're desperate. There's nothing wrong with that kind of ambition, but what hallucination-inducing drug was I taking to think that I would bypass a label mate like that? If I'd been thinking logically, I would have flooded Slick with solid beats and perhaps gained the attention of Jeezy by first supplying his label mate with heat.

As a matter of fact, this is exactly what Dow and Hen of Tha Bizness did to secure some of their first major placements. A contact of theirs invited them to a 50 Cent video shoot back when 50 Cent was on his meteoric rise to the top. At that video shoot, they recognized that it was unlikely they were going to get to the megastar himself, but they noticed a couple of hungry G-Unit members, as well as Nate Dogg (RIP), who were available. Instead of employing my idiot logic—I would have either dismissed these cats because nobody knew who they were yet or feared that my best beats would be wasted on a project that may not make it—Tha Bizness saw a golden opportunity.

They pulled these MCs (and Nate) to the side and unloaded their catalog of heat like a dump truck, eventually going on to secure placements on albums by Banks, Buck, and 213. Of course, with such smart thinking, their work led them down a path where they were eventually able to work with 50. That's how you do it! You have to keep your eye open for the cats on the way up and have enough heat in your catalog for these artists so that if a track is a miss, you can keep moving without worrying about it.

Several years before the Slick and Jeezy encounter, my terrible thinking originated from an encounter with a talented, Chicago-based producer who eventually became one of my professors of production. It was a brisk, Chicago winter night. The snow-covered sidewalks were tinted yellow by the dim streetlamps lining the block. The night looked like a winter scene from an old oil painting. Eddie Bronco and I were sitting in a worn SUV going through this producer's catalog of records. He played song after song, each more incredible than the one before it, and I sat in the back seat of his truck, locked on to his speakers like a missile, making sure no note was missed. The producer had been recording songs with local Chicago talent, and I vividly remember sitting there, shifting my thoughts from how great the music was to my anger that this music was being lost on unknown artists, going unheard outside of a tight Chicago circle. I thought it was a damn shame, so much good music vanishing into time. I vowed I would not make the same mistake. I had to save my heat for the best and use those tracks for opportunities with the widest audience possible. With that vow, the handcuffing commenced.

REALIZATION

We should all be magnetized by our ambition, but realistically, it was very unlikely that I was going to come from the depths of the unknown and place a record on a major artist's album. Why? *Because I needed to first build steam.* Instead of coveting my precious work, I should have been giving those bangers away for cheap or for free so I could build my brand and *make some noise! You have to make noise!* Just like the producer from Chicago was properly doing.

Focus tells the story of how he became an Aftermath producer:

> I was in Atlanta at the time. I was working with Jason Weaver and this company, Boob Tube, and this cat that he was working with by the name of Daks. Dre had [an] interest in Daks, and at the time, I was the only one producing Daks's project. All the songs they played for Dre were mine, and Dre was digging what we were doing together.
>
> It's funny because the first major placement that you asked me about was me and Daks on *The Wash* soundtrack. Dre was like, "I'm looking for producers, I'm looking for new blood, and I wanna know if you're ready." And I was like, "Ready to do what?" [and] he was like, "Ready to work." And I was like, "Hell, yeah!" He was like, "That's all I need to hear," and he put me in the studio that day. I literally left where we met at and went straight to the studio.

Being wise enough to work with the artist on the way up, the artist within his reach, led to the opportunity of a lifetime. Who knows what would have happened if Focus had been all about holding on to

that music for a future opportunity with a perceived
big artist?

Wisely spreading your music in every direction that
you can means that eventually somebody's going to
hear your phenomenal production. If you can't get to
so-and-so artist or A&R guy, you don't just sit there
and wait, throwing your music in a safe, waiting for
some major label opportunity. You can't handcuff
the music for opportunities that may never manifest.
You make noise with what's at your immediate disposal. People will hear you, especially with the ease
of finding new music today. If you've sharpened your
skills, you will be heard. If you're mastering your
craft, *you will continue to produce music of that caliber.*
And the most beautiful of questions will pour forth
from their lips—

"*Who produced that?*"

followed by an emphatic:

"*Damn!*"

As Hen puts it,

> Unless it's like a full song that you're holding on
> to that you know is a hit record, that's a different
> thing. If it's just a track, and you don't even know
> how it's gonna end up as a full record, it's only 50
> percent of the problem. Why hold on to it? Even
> if you had a great idea for how the song should go
> and the hook or whatever, in these days and times,
> you just gotta throw it out there ...; you don't know
> what's gonna happen. *And if you know that you can*

*create something just as good another day, then be that
confident.*

You simply never know what a track will do or how
far an artist, whether you expect it or not, can take it.

Focus recalls,

> There are several times [when] that has happened
> to me. I held on to it, and a couple of times, I got
> it to the artist I wanted to get it to and it didn't do
> crap. So, now I don't hold on to anything because
> you never know who's gonna be that overnight
> success.... You never know now, so I don't hold on
> to anything, I'm not married to anything.

> I might have a vision for a beat. For example, the
> "Respect My Conglomerate" beat that I did for
> Busta—I didn't see it for Busta, I saw it for Dre. I
> did it for *Detox*, but Busta was like, "Gimme that
> record, and I'll make it a movie," and he sat on it for
> a little while because he wanted to make sure it was
> perfect. Busta is a perfectionist himself, too, but he
> sat on it for a while, and I started getting pissed
> because I was like, "Look, I know [that] if I can
> just get the right person to write the right hook...."
> But Busta turned around and came back and was
> like, "Look, I wrote a movie to this record and it's
> done, this is gonna be a hit," and he delivered. So I
> never hold anything back. [If] Bus comes up to me
> and says, "I want that," [I'll be] like, "This don't
> even sound like you ... go ahead, take it."

Confidence

When novice producers handcuff their music like I
did, it's often deeply rooted in a lack of confidence.

(There's that damn confidence again. It just won't go away, will it?) I wasn't confident in my ability to bang out high-caliber tracks on a consistent basis. Knowing this, I subconsciously went into survival mode and shoved my best tracks in the safe. They became rare jewels, jewels I wasn't certain I could ever mine again. Will used to say, "If you think that's the best beat you're ever going to make, then you may as well quit now." That's some damn good advice.

When you're constantly improving your product, you'll gain the confidence that prevents this kind of behavior. If you've created one banger, you're more than capable of creating another. Use the information in this book and push your creativity daily until you're making those bangers more frequently. Eventually, you'll cook up a banger once a month, then bi-weekly, then weekly, until you reach that sweet spot where you're a consistent and prolific monster. You then gain enough confidence to throw your material at a variety of projects to see what sticks, without being shackled to your fear of the creative well running dry.

THE FINAL MIX

Many years ago, I ran into Wonder (one of the production geniuses behind "What You Know" by T.I.), an excellent producer more talented than famous, and I remember picking his brain for advice on how to come up in the game. He told me about some producers who were popping at the moment who basically gave all their music away for free and created a lot of noise. One day somebody came along and said, "Yo, what do you guys charge for beats?" The producers looked at each other in confusion; they didn't have a clue. But because they had the vision to give their tracks away and were willing to make as many artists sound as hot as possible, regardless of how big those artists were, they eventually created enough noise and reached a point where they were in demand. Where there is demand, there is commerce. Where there is commerce, there is potential profit.

> We look at our track record, and we look at the history of how we worked with artists. They never pick the ones that we think is our shit. We may bang it for a day or a week or so, you might hold on to it for a little bit, but after a while ... it's all good, and we just gotta let it go. —Dow

REO chimed in with his experience with handcuffing beats:

> It's definitely a tough thing to go through because you make something with someone in mind and hope it will get to them and come out, but then you also run the risk that it may never see the light of day. It's just tough. I've been in positions where I made something with someone definitely in mind and actually got to play it for them and they didn't

budge. It's like, at least I know, because I know a lot of other people never get that opportunity.

I've also been in positions where I've made something for somebody and other people wanted it, and I said no, and then when I got in place with the artist, they took it. Then, I've been in positions where I've made something with nobody in mind and somebody I had no idea was gonna like it, loved it.

So it can really go any which way. You just have to kind of use your gut. That's the only thing I can really say; use your gut. My friend told me that beats can be like groceries: they sit in the fridge too long, they can become stale or outdated, and if you're not careful, you could hold on to something for too long, you know. *The main goal is to get the music out.* —REO of the Soundkillers

Side Note: The Benefit of the Digital Age

Is there a better time in the history of music for producers to lace independent artists, of all genres, with heat? I mean, we're in the midst of the weakening of the majors; independent artists are coming up, building their own movements and fan bases, and because of social networking and the Internet, anybody can hear new music if they search for it. This is the time to sharpen your gut instincts about which artists are headed for the stars and collaborate!

LAW 9

I Want the Truth: Tap into the Real Reasons Behind Your Actions

Rationalization: I'm not gonna go to this conference. There probably won't be anybody worth meeting, and I might mess up my cash flow if I go.

Reality: *I'm not really worried about the money. If I had to, I'd find a way. I'm really trying to psych myself out of going and I'm giving excuses. If I don't give it my best, I can't really fail, can I?*

OBSERVATION

After reading several great books on how our minds work and the ways that we tend to communicate with ourselves, I learned about how we humans often think deceptive thoughts to protect ourselves. To keep ourselves nestled safely within our comfort zones, we rationalize, and the conversations we have with ourselves seem to make perfect sense. This is how people who do silly shit can rationalize it with ease and later come to realize, after the desired activity has commenced and concluded, that they have in fact done something stupid. What does this have to do with being a producer, you ask? Everything.

I remember choosing not to join beat battles because I'd heard a colleague refer to them as a waste of time. He believed that none of these battles were earning producers checks; therefore, what was the point? The same producers were there week after week without a placement. By using the process I just described, I quickly agreed and easily convinced myself that this argument was rational, so I never bothered to join a beat battle.

Deep in the back of my mind was an entirely different thought process. Remember earlier when I discussed the power of fear and what it can do to the producer's journey? I was terrified of learning that I was nowhere as hot as I thought, a discovery that would have been a steel wrecking ball hurtling through the foundation of my ego. That fear allowed my conscious mind to rationalize that "logical" decision while cleverly burying the true emotional intent of my heart, fear. I was trying to protect myself. And in trying to protect myself, I cheated myself out of the growth and progression you get from getting properly smashed in a beat battle.

The same "software conversation" took place when it was time to play beats for people as well. Without realizing it, I would rationalize and gravitate to the individuals I assumed would dig my style, instead of sacrificing myself to the judgment of people who would get into the tracks and rip them up, thus allowing me to improve.

REALIZATION

When it came time to showcase my beats, I manipulated my thoughts and actions to save myself and then convinced myself that it made sense. Understand that you may do the same, thinking thoughts that are not in your best interest. You have to tap into another part of yourself that asks, "Why am I really making this decision? Why am I not entering this showcase? Why am I not going to this conference? Why don't I ask random people what they think of my music instead of asking my yes-men friends? Why am I not shaking hands with everybody at this industry event? Am I subconsciously afraid of failure? Or even more confusing, am I afraid of success? Am I trying to sabotage myself, and I don't even realize it?"

You must know that your rational mind and emotional mind are extremely powerful tools, and you must learn how they both work for and against you. And this concept extends far beyond making music and showcasing your art to the world. This "knowing of the true self" reaches into every part of your existence. Know that the seeking of pleasure and avoidance of pain are the dominating motivators of life, and these primal desires will take you off course, set you back—or take you to the stars if you learn how to understand and use them. Listen to yourself, learn when you have a tendency to psych yourself out, and use the results to make sure you're making the right moves when it comes to your music.

THE FINAL MIX

Rationalization: This is my style, so I'm gonna send these beats despite what they asked for. If they can't see the genius behind them, their loss.

Reality: My ego is really out of control, and I think I have free rein to do what I want as a producer. I know better, but I'm not going to change.

Rationalization: I'm not gonna bother sending these beats out to these cats. I mean, I know they know music, but they'll probably never get back to me anyway; I know they're busy dudes.

Reality: I'm terrified they're going to tell me I suck. I can't handle that right now, so I'm going to sit on these tracks until I feel I've gotten better. I just spent months working on this music; I'd be devastated to hear that it isn't any good.

Rationalization: Why do I need new software? I'm pretty good with this program. It doesn't feel like a necessity.

Reality: I'm scared of having to start from scratch with a new program. It took me long enough to fig- ure out this one. They've got producers making hits on anything, so why do I have to step up to more powerful software?

Rationalization: I'm gonna take my time with this beat game. I don't want to go hard because I might burn myself out.

Reality: *I'm actually much more comfortable going half speed because I'm terrified of going hard and failing. At this rate, I know I'm not really giving it my all, so I can't really fail at becoming a producer.*

Rationalization: There are a lot of cats at this industry event, and I know I should be passing these tracks out. Everybody seems to know each other, and I don't know a soul. They'll never listen anyway. I'm just wasting my time, so I'm gonna go home.

Reality: *I don't want this nearly as badly as I think I do. But instead of being honest with myself and saying that, I'm going to go ahead and rationalize my leaving by focusing on the worst outcome—that they'll never listen—instead of focusing on the pos-sibility—that I might make some headway tonight. But I'm full of it. So I won't even go through that thought process.*

At some point in your career, you may have found yourself glued between some of those kinds of thoughts. The resulting decisions seem to make so much sense at the time. It's so easy to agree with your rationalizing mind and go home, or not buy the ticket, or avoid sending the beat. Train yourself to look beyond your fears, to be objective with yourself, to see the actions you're supposed to take.

Many of you don't have a problem with getting into a beat battle or showcase. This may not be the area where you try to hustle yourself out of something you need to do. This was just an example of where I hustled *myself*. So my questions to you are: Where in your production career are you hustling yourself? In what areas of your career are you able to rationalize bad decisions? How are you able to sweet-talk yourself out of something you know deep down you need to do? If you don't address this stuff, you suddenly look up and realize that you weren't honest with yourself about quite a few things. Then you find yourself breathing hard, lagging at the back of the marathon as a result.

Side Note: The Beat Battle

While we're on the subject of beat battles, let's discuss them for a second. Beat battles come and go. Some are interesting and entertaining, and some are deathly boring. Remember, you don't simply enter a beat battle, lose or win, and go home. A beat battle is a hammer, a tool, and it's your responsibility to build something with it. It's a means to an end. You should be extremely methodical and strategic about how you want to use these events.

Always keep in mind *who* is at a beat battle. At one of the last beat battles I attended before leaving Atlanta, Needlz and Focus were competing and entertaining the crowd. Now let's say I didn't know these cats personally and was just an average Joe trying to get in the game—best believe I would have been at these cats looking for mentoring. Who's in the crowd? Who's judging? Who's taping the show to put it on YouTube? Do they have your producer name to put in the tags?

With a beat battle, you have a free listening session, so maximize the opportunity. Make the battle work for you and your own progress. It's a stepping stone upward, not a place to feed your ego because you whupped ass or sulk because you got your ass whupped. Too many producers are entering these events only to have their egos stroked so they can feel good on the stage for a minute. There's nothing wrong with having a roomful of people appreciating and cheering for your music. That's a damn good feeling. But that's not the only reason you're there—you're at work.

Use the opportunity to gauge where you are musically. Typically, you're going to be grouped with sixteen producers. You should be listening to each of them intently to figure out how to better develop your own music. This is your chance to peek at your classmate's test to see what bubbles he's filling in. If you're not the hottest of the sixteen, then you've got work to do. You've got work to do *even if you are* the hottest. Either way, you should be leaving the venue, racing home to get back to the studio to put that motivation to use and incorporate what you learned that night. Remember, it's a tool.

During Chuck's interview, he explained that in basketball, you can find a court in any part of the country, get into a pick-up game, and gauge where your skills are. He said that the beat battle is the closest thing you have to that pick-up game. If you're out in the first round, you know you've got a long-ass way to go toward making music that reflects who you are and resonates with the masses.

If you win, you're doing some things right. More specifically, you can be comfortable knowing that your style bangs. "[It's about] really knowing who you are so that you're confident enough to stand behind your sound," says Hen. One of the best gifts you can give yourself as a beatmaker or producer is confidence in your own particular style of music. So many times I go to beat battles and everybody sounds exactly the same because a lot of producers haven't learned how to be themselves, are scared to be themselves, or haven't realized the value of being themselves. For a young producer, it can be difficult to both find your sound and trust in it, and the inability to do so can make you "sonically insecure" without your realizing it. As a result, you don't investigate and invest in what makes you unique, and instead, you simply recreate what's perceived as popular. At beat battles, sonic insecurity manifests as boredom: judges fiddling with their cell phones, checking Twitter and Facebook, waiting for the next round. Take Hen's advice. Examine your sound, pay attention while you're mastering your craft, and give yourself the confidence to stand behind your sound.

During your battles, analyze your competitors, use the competition as inspiration, incorporate their progressions, sounds, and melodies, mimic their drums, dissect their mixes. You may have paid good money to enter the competition. Get your money's worth.

Part 3: What Should I Understand?

LAW 10

Pay the Cost to Be the Boss: Earn the Title
"Producer," Don't Just Declare It

OBSERVATION

I made a grave mistake by misinterpreting what I
was supposed to be doing if I had the gall to declare
that I was a *producer*. I didn't realize that the term
"producer" is something you earn, not something
you declare. Instead, I was a novice beatmaker, sitting in my room banging out track after track. As the
months turned to years, my ignorance built a fence
in front of my ability to transition from bedroom
beatmaker extraordinaire to producer, a fence that
prevented me from understanding what a producer
was supposed to really be and do. And honestly, *I got
comfortable doing the minimum*. (Sometimes, that's
what I believe staying a beatmaker is all about. You
start making tracks and get comfortable with that
level of responsibility, that level of effort. Stepping
off the ledge into producer-land represents a whole
new world of responsibilities and concepts to master,
and you just spent five years trying to figure out how

to be a beatmaker. I think that it's an unconscious decision that one can make: *This is good enough for me right now.*)

REALIZATION

Today's beatmaker has been overrun by a gazillion other beatmakers. Because of the advancements in recording and production technology, the barriers to entry have been demolished like the Berlin Wall. The result looks like a bloody scene from a zombie flick. An unseen contagion, the production bug, infiltrates a raucous crowd of normal music lovers. The infected start convulsing violently, transformed by the lust and appeal of music production into something inhuman. Now, as drooling, flesh-eating undead, they begin to gorge on the living, one by one. In a matter of minutes, one zombie infects two more, and the infection spreads until hordes of biting, clawing monsters have flooded the streets, locking their beady eyes on any tender morsel of an artist ready to buy a beat for $2.99. Control is lost, chaos takes over, zombies are everywhere, and suddenly it's nearly impossible to make a living.

Now that so many people produce, this is your world. Within this new world, it's difficult to find a way to stand out, to be special. Yet some eventually do find a way. Who might those be? The beatmakers who evolve into producers. Because not only can a producer do what a beatmaker can do in terms of sitting in his bedroom making a hot-ass track, but a producer also has writers on deck. The producer is instrumental in formulating concepts for his records so his clients don't have to think about it. The producer sells the track with a vision, a song, or a hook, and the manager or A&R or artist has nothing to do but nod his head and say, "Oh yeah, that's hot. We'll take that one." The producer is invested in the complete process of developing that record. He's knowledgeable of the song mechanics of the genre and market he's dealing with. He knows what sounds are trending, what styles, formats, and BPMs are current. He knows what the tastemakers are looking for. He knows how to do his homework beforehand so he can take the proper material into a session and give an artist exactly what he needs. He knows how to produce the vocals of the scratch vocalist or artist, or he's smart enough to work with someone who can do this with him. He has developed an ear for matching sound: this song with that artist, this style with that pop singer, this change of sonic direction at that point in an artist's career.

REO says,

> Personally, I think there's a big difference between beatmaking and producing that isn't really discussed very often. A producer usually has the vision to carry out a full song, from the track to the vocals, all the way to the final master. You

have to ask yourself, do you have the vision to be in the studio with a songwriter and help produce the vocals, or help with harmonies, or help change a melody? If there isn't an engineer, are you able to get in the chair and engineer a session?

For example, you and a songwriter start and finish a record; you find out an artist wants to cut it. You then go to the session with the songwriter and he's asking you about what backgrounds to add. If you don't have any knowledge about that, you have to do your research. You have to get knowledgeable about it, or you're going to be that person where people are like, "Don't hire them, we'll have to do everything."

You don't have to know how to play or write every part yourself, but the artist is depending on the producer to have a vision for the final product. There are so many parts involved in producing a finished record besides the beat. If you're sending beats to a rapper, he jumps on it and releases it; okay, you made a beat, but you didn't actually produce the song. It's just a term they use on the credits. The more you get into this game, especially if you're doing R&B and pop music, you really have to produce, like, for real. I think that's why a lot of times some of these big guys get a lot of beatmakers under them, and then they end up producing records while the kid just makes the beat.

The beatmaker, lacking in skill and experience, may not have that kind of weaponry at his disposal.

Avoid my mistake. I saw the signs on the icy road warning of imminent danger, and I ignorantly kept driving down my comfortable beatmaker road. I remember picking up on little things from my production friends: "Yeah, man, I'm getting in the studio with this songwriter over here," "I got my girl putting down a hook on this beat," "We're helping such and such shape her demo." Those words flew into one ear, traveled swiftly through the hollow cavern in between, and out the other ear.

What I should have been catching was that it was time for me to step out of my self-erected fort and collaborate with some songwriters. It was time to expand my musical palette instead of making East Coast–flavored rap beats over and over again. It was time to get into the studio and paint concepts around those beats. Instead of sitting around, praying that someone would place my beats on a major release, I should have started working with artists within my reach, learning to coax the best out of them, and *ultimately delivering a great song and not just a good beat.* I definitely saw a vision for many of my tracks. But the vision doesn't go with you when you drop off your beat CD for a busy A&R person.

See the warning signals. Open your ears. The Neptunes are on my list of the top three producers ever. What Pharrell Williams and Chad Hugo have done in the industry and the way they're able to produce records and work with artists is incredible. You've seen the videos online, haven't you? An artist comes in, they vibe with him, a concept emerges, lyrics begin to form, music manifests into a track, and together they create magic. If your goal is to become a professional producer, the Neptunes represent one of the most incredible models to study. And don't be discouraged by the completeness of their workflow. Not everyone is equipped with the full spectrum of gifts and talents to create such magic alone, but remember that being a producer doesn't mean you have to work by yourself. It's actually supposed to be the opposite. Form a team. You think all of the major producers you're looking up to are sitting there alone, cooking up all of that deliciousness you hear on the radio? Negative. Many times, there's a whole team working in the kitchen with them. And they're getting checks, too.

Today's Producer

I would be remiss if I didn't discuss the notion of being a producer in today's music business. We all know that recording budgets have been hacked to death like young, nubile teenagers in a Jason horror flick. We know that the days of producers actually getting into the studio with artists to work on material is going the way of the dinosaur and reserved only for the elite and "it" producers of the moment. Often, you'll be e-mailing a session. So what are you supposed to do when you're trying to be a producer and the industry has relegated many to beatmaker status? I love the wisdom I received from Dow and Hen regarding being full producers under these current circumstances. Hen says,

> For us, …we understand that things do change, and the way that music [is] even being made has completely changed, but we understand we wanted to be producers of the old age, where you were overseeing projects, you were helping [to] create sounds…. We always keep that in the back of our minds, even when we're just shopping tracks to cats over e-mail or through iChat or whatever. So that's when you have beats that *stand out like full production.*

Their solution to not always being able to get in the studio with artists is to consciously construct music that, to them, is *fully* produced. They strive to make the product so complete and precise in terms of what that artist is looking for that the music stands tall without their physically being there: "You're just trying to create that feeling so that even when you're not there, it can autopilot produce itself. Because the music will generally take that artist into that lane," says Hen. Develop those beats and songs to the point where there's no other outcome but taking somebody where they need to go. Make the music represent you like you're in the room. Make every ear in that studio feel your presence as if you were in there nodding your head, using your enthusiasm to sell the track to them in person. *Have a well-constructed, fully produced product.*

THE FINAL MIX

Let's not discount the beatmaker. That's not my goal at all. Chuck Greene told me years ago that you must learn to run before you can fly. In other words, first become the best beatmaker you can be, and then move on to producing when the time is right. Make those beats and get damn good at it. Stack and build your library of heat. But remember, this may only be a stop in your track trek, with more to grow, more to do, and more to become.

Do your best to find some mentors in your area. It's strange—we come up as creators of music, and many of us don't get the opportunity to witness the wide-angle, high-def view of a producer's talents, skills, and responsibilities. Deny yourself the comfort of sitting in your own studio day after day, and find someone more knowledgeable than you whom you can sit with, intern with, or watch to see how a producer does what he does.

You have to learn what happens after the beat is made or the hook is written. How do you coach artists in the booth to get the best possible songs? How do you maintain the studio session, make artists comfortable, and get the best out of them? How do you manage those big egos and personalities in the room? How do you know which songwriters would be perfect for which tracks and artists? When it comes to vocal production, how do you know which key the singers should be singing in, how the harmony sections should be produced? Can you suitably engineer tracks and work the pro-tools session if there isn't an engineer available?

You may be in a situation where you have to wear multiple hats—will you be prepared? You don't want to know how it feels to have an artist, manager, crew, or label rep glaring at you with frustration, shooting darts of death as you bumble around the console wasting time and money in a session. They'll talk about you as soon as they get a chance. You don't want to land the opportunity to get in the studio with an expert songwriter and she's looking at you like you have two heads because you can't tell her what key to work in or she has to sit in your place and re-produce the record because your arrangement is all wrong (don't be surprised when she wants some of your publishing for doing your job). That's a relationship that could have blossomed. Instead, that songwriter won't be interested in working with you again.

If you seek to become a real producer, do your best to practice your craft beforehand. You can't sit in your favorite chair in your living room, sipping a brew, and whisper proudly to yourself, "I'm just like

Rocky," without running up the stairs at 5 a.m. and sparring with hanging cow carcasses. If you want the title, earn it. If you're comfortable being a beatmaker, and that's what you want to become proficient at, there's nothing wrong with that. Just be conscious of which path you choose to walk. Don't be like me and suddenly find yourself pulled over on the side of a random road with the map fully unfolded, confused, trying to figure out how the hell you got where you are.

One thing I noticed while writing this book is that producers use the word "beatmaker" like a bigot uses a racial slur. All day, all over the social networks, producers and beatmakers are flinging the term "beatmaker" back and forth at each other, trying to separate themselves from the novices and brand themselves as the guys who are *producing* and not *just making beats.* So, I ask three questions: (1) Are you wasting your breath calling out the next man when you could focus instead on sharpening your own production skills? (2) Are you separating yourself verbally by referring to yourself as a producer, only to go home and do beatmaker things, having no concept of some of those responsibilities I've mentioned here? (3) If I put all of you "producers" in a studio with Gaga, Bruno Mars, or Andre 3000 and told you to develop a hot record, fully produced and mixed, could you do it?

Being a beatmaker is enough to get you in the door. But five or ten years later, will you be able to keep juggling the music-industry balls? That's why this information is so important. This transformation from beatmaker to producer doesn't affect most of you who are focused on cracking through the doors of the business now, but it will affect you down the road when you need versatility and true skill to build longevity.

I'll conclude this chapter with the wisdom of two Platinum producers, Troy Taylor and Focus, both of whom come from a different era than I regarding the term "producer." Troy recalls,

> I knew what a producer was, because I was a Quincy Jones fan, so I knew that even if you weren't playing the music, you still were responsible for putting the right people together to make the music. So, either way, you were being a producer. The term "beatmaker" really evolved because as soon as the technology got better—well, better or more sophisticated—I think that's what people started doing; they started spending more time making beats and not writing songs and arranging songs to those tracks. So, it really became just about tracks.

> Me, I was a songwriter, [so] whenever I made the track, I wrote the song as I was going along, so I was doing it all at once. I didn't know [any] other way; *I didn't know to be comfortable with just making a track, so, now you're a producer.* I was the all-in-one, the 100 percent, as they say. If the song got sold, I was the one that was gonna go in there *and*

> *produce and make sure that you followed the guidelines … I laid down.* I didn't know any other way. This make-a-track-and-now-you're-a-producer thing is really crazy.

I didn't know to be comfortable with just making a track, so now you're a producer. Interesting. Interesting, indeed.

Focus reflects,

> Now remember, Quincy Jones did *Thriller,* and if you look at all the documentaries, do you see him playing any instruments? Producers turned around and composed and arranged, and he conducted the orchestra and he wrote, but he didn't play any instruments. Now we have the producer playing the instruments, which back in those days, we were just studio-session instrumentalists or session players called in, or programmers. But now "programmer" and "producer" are synonymous. You have to perfect your craft, learn what you're doing, learn how to arrange vocals. Stop using the standard voices in your keyboard and start to find real voices and tweak 'em. *Make 'em sound like you.* Don't sample a snare from Timbaland and think that you're the bomb. Find the original sample that maybe Timbaland got it from and tweak it a different way. Learn how to EQ your stuff, learn how to use your compressors, *understand that stuff.*

I hope you now have a solid understanding of the difference between beatmakers and producers, and I hope that you'll use the term "producer" only after you've earned it. Most important, I hope I've motivated you to want to earn it, to want to master the abilities that separate beatmaker from producer, the abilities that build the foundation of a long career and make you unique among the competition.

LAW 11

Deaf Jam: Beware of the Danger of Sound Isolation

It's bigger than just having a cool beat; you gotta have the right beat for the right artists. —Dow, Tha Bizness

OBSERVATION

Because I was living such an isolated production life, eventually I began to lose track of my own sound and of what was commercial or currently marketable. Sitting in my home studio each day, I ultimately began building, concrete block by concrete block, a creative box for myself, and as a willing resident of this box, I couldn't see its walls (I call this the producer's self-constructed sound-deprivation box).

A wake-up call came when, through a rare wise chess move, I invited my boys Ric and Dia from Sweatbeatz Productions to come through and critique my beats. They began the process of systematically analyzing and tearing down my tracks (not me!) and unexpectedly made me realize that all of my beats were using a repetitive structure and format. They said that my drum programming and drum sound selection needed serious work and that, most important, I was creating an underground hip-hop sound that I had no intention of creating. I wanted to sound like radio-ready Just Blaze; instead, here I was sounding like a gritty, underground backpacker. Stuck inside this box, I'd lost the ability to be critical of my own music, an ability essential to constantly progressing as a producer.

REALIZATION

Once I was made aware that my production style was driving underground and sounding less mainstream, the critique was shocking enough to make me better scrutinize my sounds, diversify my drum patterns, and assess the commercial viability of my product. I realized that my individual drum selections and repetitive sequencing arrangements were contributing to this underground sound I wasn't aiming for. I learned that day that *the sum of your production parts equals your production whole*. When you blindly choose certain drums and structures, you can end up creating a sound that you didn't intend to create.

When I spoke with Needlz about his journey into producing, he revealed that he actually started as a DJ. He gave some valuable insight into what we're discussing when he explained that as a DJ, "You're basically a psychologist. Every song you play, you have to look up and see the reaction. You gotta pay attention to what the crowd is telling you. [It's the] same thing with making beats. I know a certain snare is gonna get a certain feel to different people." It's amazing that even the individual drum sounds we choose play such a huge role in our sound, our potential market demographic, and whom we should shop tracks to. Needlz pointed out that "9th [Wonder] uses that same snare because it connects to his demographic; [it's] just the little nuances of producing that satisfy the customer." Needlz' quote reflects how critical you'll need to be when selecting sounds and constructing your music.

Like Good Chefs Can Assess Their Own Meals

As difficult as it is to self-analyze your production level, it's even more challenging to break down the elements of your own music to pinpoint *where* you have holes in your game. Drums, mixing, chord progressions, melodies, sound selection—there are so many individual ingredients within the overall recipe that you have to be able to taste individually. You have to be able to sample the meal and realize that you overcooked the rice (intros are too long), you were heavy-handed with the seasoning on the steak (your 808, kick, and bass line are muddy), or the meal's flavors are imbalanced (you need to fix your arrangements for better song structure). As you assess your own product, get granular. Dissect your music; gain deep insight into each of the flavors of your meal.

Make sure to benchmark against both talented amateurs and professionals, and be as vigilant and perceptive as you can so you can learn to pinpoint your own mistakes in your recipe. Once you can scrutinize those ingredients and comprehend where you need to add and where you need to scale back, you'll be in a better position to more accurately cook up the entire exquisite meal.

Your Sound and Market

Are you following in my footsteps, thinking that you're exempt from analyzing the commercial viability of your product? Ready for the checks, but you just want to focus on the creative parts, and think the rest of that stuff is irrelevant, huh? Not even what it is, player. As a producer aspiring to success, you must be acutely aware of the markets in which your tracks reside.

Certain drum and sound selections work well with certain genres. Certain chord structures and progressions match certain styles of music. For example, the I IV V progression is well known in popular music. Different variations of that progression dominate the charts because they bring a familiar, positive vibe to the listener. You'll tend to score bigger with tracks that incorporate the feel of that progression when you're shopping to mainstream pop artists. Knowing this, when you get the opportunity to shop a track in that vein, you send something that the pop artist and consumer can relate to instead of a super-chopped, grimy soul sample. Now, don't get me wrong, there's nothing wrong with the super-chopped, grimy soul sample, but those records aren't typically the most commercial. If that's what you do, then cool, but you shouldn't send that out when a pop diva is looking for Top 40 material. These are the subtle elements of being a producer that you miss when you're stuck in novice beatmaker mode in your sound prison.

The Alchemist is one of my favorite producers. I see production as a kind of telepathy: the unique way that a producer composes music can touch a listener in a very precise way. It's like the brain waves of both maker and user equate, with each communicating via the same musical language. The way The Alchemist makes music—we speak the same beat dialect. If you're familiar with Al's work, he excels with rich, often grimy soul samples, moody progressions, and dark, cinematic sounds. Al's beats hit the streets like a jackhammer. Timbaland, one of the greatest producers of our generation, doesn't hit the streets with quite the same force, but the records you get from Tim will collectively hypnotize popular culture, sending people to iTunes to click "buy" like zombies. Typically, you don't go to Al for a Top 40 pop record and you don't go to Tim for a gutter track (though obviously, with such skill, they'd be more than capable). Typically, what should people be coming to you for?

Dow put it perfectly when he told me,

> The same hustle you have in making your beats, you gotta have the same hustle in getting them off and finding ways to get them off. Who's the right person to get them off to? If you're doing some Flo Rida–type beats, there's no point in trying to take that shit to Jeezy; he doesn't wanna hear that shit and vice versa. You gotta know who you're playing stuff for. And we see a lot of producers now, they just have no idea.... "This beat's tight to me," but it doesn't fit who they're playing for and they'll wonder, like, "Yo! Why doesn't anybody mess with me?"

Don't think you're the club guy if your beats sound hard and dirty. Don't think you're going to get a phone call from Rick Ross if you've got a production style that lies in the vein of Justin Bieber. You don't e-mail Black Eyed Peas records when Action Bronson is looking for music. I know these examples sound ridiculous; however, I've seen this a million times, and sadly, these examples are not silly or uncommon. You'd be appalled at the level of market ignorance out there. I've been on the receiving end of hundreds of beats that were nowhere near the sound of the intended prospect. In my experience with music licensing, the Music Dealers A&R department often receives music that has nothing at all to do with the brief. Receiving gritty tracks for a rapper when you asked for something futuristic for a pop singer always baffles us. I never know if people are ignorant or if they just don't care. Maybe they're so hungry that they assume that something sent in is better than nothing. I would disagree. Don't insult the people who took time to give you a listen by bombarding them with a style that has nothing to do with them. Do your due diligence. Mistakes like that reveal that you're not taking your craft seriously. Yes, you should have a style. Yes, you should push your creative boundaries. But no, you shouldn't haphazardly come out of nowhere with music that doesn't fit the intended prospect. Study artists' discographies to get an accurate sense of their styles. *Take your own ego out of the equation.*

Honest Talent Self-Assessment

I want to quickly elaborate on another danger that comes with putting yourself in the sound-deprivation box: a producer's inability to understand his level of talent. I suffered from this, and *many* of you suffer from this problem as well. How do I know? I, as well as most industry professionals, receive countless beat CDs from producers who end their pitches with "Dude, this is the hottest shit in the streets, you're gonna love it, I guarantee." Don't ever, ever, ever say that. Instantly, the neurons fire in your recipient's brain, summoning with vivid detail the memory of every other producer who made the same declaration upon handing over a beat CD, and 95 percent of the time it was trash. Let the music make the declaration for you. Be confident in your music, but don't guarantee the absolute hottest music they've ever heard.

But I digress. Some producers are incapable of knowing where they stand in terms of their level of production skill. I haven't yet figured out how this happens given the volume of incredible music around us, but it does. I think there's something about being so close to your own art that makes it incredibly difficult to judge objectively. Regardless, you have to find a good system of understanding where you fall in terms of how ready your product is. Many of you are way off and have some years to go before you're industry-ready. Time and time again I surf through producers' bios and links on social media to listen to their music after they've declared that they're the best, the hottest, the next best thing, only to hear several years of growth ahead of them before they could *consistently* compete with placement-getters. You need to benchmark yourselves against what you hear not only from professionals, but also from extremely talented amateurs before you profess greatness. (Not to mention, modesty and humbleness go a long way in this business. Let your listeners proclaim your greatness; if you need to state your greatness, you're probably not there. Your finished work should do all the speaking for you.)

The inability to self-assess becomes hazardous when you overestimate your talent: your work is really a five, but you assume it's a ten. Then you're out there networking and hustling beats only to discover a year or two later that all that time may have been wasted because you weren't nearly as good as you *thought* you were. Instead, you should have been at home sharpening the production sword.

THE FINAL MIX

Do whatever it is you have to do to know *your* sound, what parts of your production are contributing to your overall sound, and your target market. Use your creative production breaks to create distance from your music so you an approach it with fresh, objective ears. Invite trusted producers to critique your music. Use their feedback to assess your total product as it relates to your goals. Benchmark against the leaders of your genre; how do you sound compared to them?

Unfortunately, these processes take time. Success in this area boils down to good ol'-fashioned experience developed by spending quality time with your music. But, most important, you can't even begin to tackle these ideas unless you place enough importance on the dangers of sound isolation. It sucks to see producers ignore the self-assessment of their art and watch them spin their wheels in the mud as a result. *Make sure that your vision and sound align.* You must be self-aware as a creator of music in a commercial capacity.

Side Note: The Spectrum of Amateur Talent

I remember an eye-opening experience from a time when I was privileged to sit in on a session with a lovely R&B songstress and observe a select group of amateur (and a few professional-level) producers invited to play music and pitch concepts for songs. I was utterly amazed by the quality of music being pitched. There's something about hearing skilled producers pitch instrumentals with concepts *before* they become records on the radio that *really* changes your perspective. I had to actually get up and shake people's hands for being that damn talented.

But here's what's interesting—most of those producers were still grinding to create real traction in the business. Some had placements, but as a whole, they were still relatively low on the career totem pole despite being extremely talented with polished sounds. I was blown away as I thought, "This level of quality music is coming from dudes in the same pool as everyone else fighting for a chance, *especially the same mediocre cats claiming greatness all over the Internet?*"

That session changed my perception of the skill level necessary to gain success and made me painfully

aware of just how fierce the amateur competition really is. That experience, combined with several years
of working with Dynamic Producer, substantially
raised my standards for production quality, making
them much more realistic. It also revealed just how
wide the talent spectrum for amateur producers really is. There are producers wading in the same creative
pool as you who can compose at the level of quality
and consistency of big-name producers, but they just
haven't created their shot yet.

So for any of you who are running short on humil-
ity, you fivers who can't hear what you sound like and
believe that you're tenners, keep this idea in the back
of your mind while you're out running the streets
claiming you're hotter than lava.

LAW 12

Weapons of War: Choose Your Production Style Wisely

OBSERVATION

In the winter, the University of Michigan looks like a dystopian sci-fi film where the imbalances in nature have frozen the planet, sending humans to retreat closer to the earth's core to keep warm. After the 2003 holiday break, I returned to the ice cube of Ann Arbor for my final semester of college. I was back early, with a little time before classes got cracking. It was during these first few icy days that the beatmaking God reached from the heavens with a glowing hand and ceremoniously touched me on the forehead with his index finger, anointing *me* to fully join the kingdom. Bursting with excitement, I got busy looking for a new program (in the fall, I'd gotten my feet wet by tinkering with Fruity Loops) to begin my journey through the Production Promised Land, eventually discovering software called Acid Pro.

I jumped off the springboard and dove right into sampling, digging digitally for twinkling MP3 jewels of soul and jazz classics. I chopped. I arranged. I looped. I marveled at my creations, staring at the computer screen excitedly like Dr. Victor Frankenstein noticing the twitching fingers of his freshly electrified monster. Now, knowing I was headed in the direction of production, I thought it wise to preemptively expand my creative horizons, so I signed up for a music production class in my upcoming final semester. Little did I know, this decision would begin a chain reaction of negative thinking that would cripple my ability to evolve.

As class began, I assumed that because I already had experience sampling and arranging (if you could call what I did in the month or so prior *experience*), I'd strut my ass through the front door, badass style, the way an outlaw cowboy flings open the swinging doors of a saloon, the sheer magnitude of his swagger forcing the boisterous room to melt to silence. I looked my classmates up and down. My ego bragged, "Music production, huh. Shit. The hell *you* clowns know about music production? Let me show you losers how this is done." Instead, during the first few weeks of my digital music production class, every piece of equipment in that tiny room kicked my ass. I caught a sharp elbow in the gut from the Korg keyboard. The DAW, the ring-leading goon, rained swift judo chops upon me. Midi slogged me across the jaw with a hook when I wasn't looking. It was like I'd been jumped by three blinking and bleeping thugs in a dirty alley, each laughing like evil clowns as they ran off with my confidence.

I, Mr. Cool Sampling Guy, the one who was supposed to have it all under control, awkwardly probed around that foreign production setup like a virgin trying to figure out the mechanics of pleasing a more experienced lover while she snickered in disbelief. I sat in front of my Korg keyboard, nervous and frustrated, beads of sweat accumulating on my forehead, class after class. But it wasn't all my fault per se. I had no knowledge of music theory, of playing the keys, midi, or the Korg keyboard. Adding to the chaos was Digital Performer, a pro sequencer so complex it seemed to have been designed for navigating satellites instead of making music. These were the ingredients that formed the recipe for a mental disaster.

While I was struggling, two musically trained nerds from the college's School of Music were easily banging out funky compositions, bursting with layers of tracks, melodies, and extraterrestrial sounds. Just from listening to their music, I imagined their futures: by day, they worked on the scores for the next *Halo* or *Call of Duty;* by night, sitting comfortably in their parents' basements, they stuffed themselves with Hot Pockets and invested their entire lives in *World of Warcraft*. Despite the funny visual, they could create well-composed music from scratch, and my jealousy bubbled. They were highly trained in music theory and could play the keys. So, for the most part, even if they weren't making hot beats, they understood the rules of music and composition.

REALIZATION

Class after class, I let the weight of that experience flatten my creativity and self-belief into a pitiful pancake. I'm very competitive with myself. In those brief four months of class, I became extremely shortsighted. At home, my early sampled beats were winning ooohs and aaahs, and everything I made in class sounded like crap. I couldn't envision victory as an original composer of music—no cheering crowds, no chunky checks. I only wanted to play in an arena where I thought I could win big. Instead of existing in that state of poor creative output, after that class, I intentionally avoided original beats and committed myself to sampling in my MPC, where I thought I could be a champion.

The negative thinking from this experience ate through my creative mind, hampering my development in the process. I hope that you'll never question what you're capable of. If you've got the music in your heart, find a way to get it out. The good Lord wouldn't give you the desire if he didn't also give you the means to express it. Sign up for a music theory or piano class *now* and get it in. (Feeling like a complete idiot on the keys inspired me to take piano lessons for a good few months after I graduated so I could at least play along with my sampled beats. I managed to form a foundation that would eventually help me years later when I did regain the courage to get back on the keyboard.)

Not to mention, as I think back on that class, I was a moron to believe I was going to be great at creating original music in only four months. I mean, up until that point, I had about as much experience writing music as I had breathing underwater. I must have thought that as my fingertips hovered above the keyboard, a glowing, sparkling energy of com-position and digital production skill would magically transfer from the keys up through my hands and arms into my brain via my ears. After this transfer, I'd take one deep breath, then effortlessly wiggle my fingers and create music like a savant. Obviously, this was not the case. My impatience was legendary. My expectation of myself was incredible. I didn't even give myself the proper chance to evolve. I greatly underestimated the time it took to even scratch the wide surface of my own creativity.

To all of my sample kings and queens, be cautious of any experiences or thought patterns that keep you from making an earnest attempt at creating original music. Use this chapter to understand what frustration and impatience can do to you and how quickly they can do it. Learning to create takes time, especially when you're untrained (there were no piano or theory lessons for me to lean on). Refuse to be stopped by your own poor thinking. As soon as those thoughts show up on your doorstep, knocking frantically to join you inside, get them out of there. There's nothing wrong with being a samplehead or an MPC king, but try not to force that style upon yourself because you assume you're incapable of anything else. Creativity takes time. And if you're already well into the keyboard game, are you working off of limited knowledge and doing the minimum? Or are you really *educating yourself* on music theory and *mastering the ability* to create dynamic, captivating progressions and melodies that mesmerize?

The Debate

I must address the underlying debate between the pros and cons of sampling vs. original production, or whether or not you can *thrive* as a sampler only, because this question was always lingering in the back of my mind when I was a self-proclaimed sample king. Sampled beats or original beats? Well, that depends on your goals, of course. Can you reach the heights of *mainstream success* and stay there as a sample-only producer? From my professional point of view, the answer is yes, but not like you could back in the day. If you stick to direct sampling only, you're cutting off a significant portion of outlets to hustle and publishing to earn. Trust me, it hurts to admit this. With each letter typed, I feel more like a rat, sweating under the bright fluorescent lights of an interrogation room, betraying my own brotherhood (hopefully no one comes to kill the stool pigeon).

First, market and consumer tastes have changed drastically. As I said earlier, I came up during an era when the *entire* album was full of samples. Lead single, sample. B-side cut, sample. Skits, sample. At least a good 90 percent of my top classic albums were chock full of samples. Supreme Clientele, Reasonable Doubt, Ready to Die, It Was Written ... the list goes on. The bosses of production were pioneers who wielded samples formidably like lumberjacks wield axes: The Alchemist, Ski Beatz, DJ Clark Kent, Trackmasters, Premier, Just Blaze, Dilla, Kanye, Pete Rock, etc., etc.! It was a musically magnificent time. Back then, sampling was so ingrained in production/hip-hop culture, original beats could kiss most people's asses.

However, today, we're playing in a different sonic arena. Have you listened to the radio lately? Pick any genre and you're likely to run into an orgy of electronic sound. The pool for sample-based opportunities, once Olympic-sized, has now shrunk down to the blow-up pool in your uncle's backyard with a seating capacity of three six-year-old girls. That might be a slight exaggeration, but there are definitely far fewer albums that are 90 percent sample-based. We have to keep it real!

Second, given the difficulty of maintaining a career, versatility has become an ever-important skill. Producers who can deliver a variety of styles, essentially whatever's needed by different types of artists and different types of opportunities, build a better chance of thriving in today's music market. The producer who can dig through the crates and sit at his MPC and chef up a banger, *and* sit at his keyboard and cook up equal hotness, significantly expands his ability to thrive. The producer who can produce a pop track, compose a gutter East Coast track, send tracks off for TV and film placement, and set aside a few tracks for video games creates more favorable financial possibilities for himself. He can put his talent into a variety of mediums and create separate revenue streams.

Third, speaking of revenue streams, the producer who only samples, well, he's getting checks that are a little lighter because he's got publishing owners and master-recording owners whipping out their shiny knives and forks to gorge on scrumptious pieces of his publishing pie. Budget cuts, difficulties clearing samples, and the lack of sampled material in sync licensing can all cut into his pockets (ask those producers you know who don't have a nine-to-five; sync licensing is a huge part of the game, and there's little room for sampled material in that arena).

Now, I'm not saying that you can't thrive being only a sample-based producer in this day and age. So not true. While most of his current production isn't built on the recognizable soul samples of his past works, I would still define Kanye West as a producer thriving from sample-based production. As well, other sample-based producers continue to thrive today; we can thank greats like 9th Wonder, Madlib, and Statik Selektah for carrying the tradition. Consider the blossoming Mashup genre, a new course for sampleheads. However, if you listen closely, there aren't nearly as many sample-only producers thriving now compared to just five or ten years ago, are there? You can still become a legend, but understand that the arena is a little smaller. If your goals involve that style and market, and you have consciously made that decision, do your thing and do it well. I want you to succeed at the style you have *consciously* chosen. All I hope is that you don't let your ego, ignorance, or fear stop you from attacking many forms of creation.

If you seek the path of production versatility, throw yourself into the keyboard and get acquainted with music theory. Train yourself to select rich sounds and instruments. Explore your creativity. Hit both the MPC and the keyboard, combine the two, and see what you can create. This is what I eventually started to do, and it became the most exciting option for me creatively. If you're starting out as a keyboard cat, reverse the situation and sample something. See what the other world is about. You'll probably inspire new creativity and come up with something crazy that you can interpolate because you've sharpened your skills.

If I'd had the wisdom then that I have now, I would have started out with piano lessons and divided my time between sampling and playing original tracks. That way I would have equally trained my original music muscles and my sampling muscles instead of looking like the guy at the gym who hammers relentlessly on his biceps while his legs look like juice-box straws.

Adjustments to the Plan

Some of my favorite sample-based producers were changing their tactics during the mid-2000s. Me, afflicted with a nasty case of production tunnel vision, I didn't even notice. Kanye, who breathed fresh life into the art of soul sampling, was slowly but surely altering his style completely, interpolating, working with musicians and other producers, evolving his sound, and moving toward tracks that were more mainstream (not to say the change in his sound was bad or good, but it was certainly changing). On the radio, you started hearing a lot less of the old East Coast, four-bar loop formula. More sample-based producers were working with musicians to re-create grooves from scratch (and cutting out some of the copyright issues). If the cats we idolize are always adjusting their game plans, what makes you think you shouldn't constantly analyze your own situation and, when it's time, adjust, too? (Notice that I said *adjust their game plans,* not change them.)

Don't do as I did and stick to one discipline for so long that you lose both the vision of what you're capable of and precious time bringing that vision to reality. There's so much you can do if you believe you can do it. As I hit that keyboard *years* later, I was absolutely amazed that I could create some of the things I created. I used to sit in my studio and think to myself, "Damn, did I make that?" And these weren't hot beats by far, they were god-awful, but to create anything when you believed you were capable of nothing was a dope experience.

The creative leap became possible only after I changed my perception of what was possible. And if you haven't, you need to do the same. Time and practice can change anything! The producers who were terrible at crafting keyboard beats yesterday are getting checks for original music for commercials today. The ones who didn't think they could do anything besides grungy hip-hop broadened their production palettes and are in the studio with pop artists. Believe; then practice your ass off.

Key to the Law: Creative Confidence

Before we move on, I just want to add one more thing to the conversation by touching on *confidence and how it relates to original music.* Let me tell you something. There's nothing like nonchalantly sitting down in the studio, not caring who's there or whether there's an artist in the room with you while you're working, and wiggling your fingers across the keyboard while transferring the musical thoughts in your mind to your fingers, and it sounds dope. There's nothing like having a songwriter come through to sing what he's written, and then you immediately map out a key and chord progression to match what he's singing.

Watching producers do this is beautiful. It's my version of watching in awe as an artist paints, effortlessly flinging the brush back and forth until something miraculous appears on the canvas. Of course, it's cool to come in with music already made, but you open an entire world of creative possibility when you can *confidently do whatever you want in the studio.* You walk with a whole new swagger. For those of us without the complete tool set, there are situations where we can feel awkward. While listening to talented producers fiddle around on the keyboard and create beautiful melodies on the spot, I've sat there with my face twisted by jealousy because I hadn't put myself in a position to do that. Because I haven't developed a solid understanding of theory and trained my ear, I have a harder time translating what I hear in my head. When I was producing, I preferred to produce by myself, tucked away, trying out different melodies and progressions until I found what I heard in my head, because I didn't know how long it would take me to come up with something, and everything before it was complete would sound like steaming crap. *Give yourself the highest level of creative confidence you can.* Practice your craft! It will feel amazing to command your art in that manner.

THE FINAL MIX

I don't want to give the impression that I think sampling is less creative or that you can't reach the heights of your career by being a sampler. I still love sampled beats, sampling is a part of who I am, and it requires creativity and genius to excel as a sample-based producer. Sampled production is still integral to the canon of popular music. However, I will acknowledge that it is more difficult to remain a sample-only producer in *this* era of music. I will also acknowledge that because of the difficulty of earning checks today, you have to analyze the financial aspects of your method of creation. The point of this law is more about producers denying abilities and skills that I'm sure they can build. I relied on samples and chose to be a sample-based producer because I never thought I'd make beats as well as I did without the use of somebody else's art. This is what I want you to avoid. Choose to be a sample-based producer because that's the only music you ever hear in your heart and you're sure there's nothing else for you. Choose to be a sample-based producer because you sincerely tried making keyboard beats and you felt it didn't suit you. To keep things in the proper perspective, Chuck Greene reminded me that "A hot record is a hot record. If it's hot and it's got a sample, it is what it is. Kanye West, he made his name off of hot samples, and he got richer than rich."

REO expressed similar sentiments in regard to hot records and samples: "At the end of the day, if you sample something, and you get 5 percent of the sample and it's a hit, 5 percent of a hit can be a lot of money, as opposed to 50 percent of an album cut. There are different ways to look at it." It doesn't matter to the market whether the record is a sample or an original track, as long as it's hot. Now keep in mind that Chuck went on to say, "There will come a point where we will say, okay, now let's relax on the sampling because you have a lot going on for you, but you're not making as much money as you could

be because you're sampling." So he shares my sentiments. And when that conversation comes in your
own career, it's your responsibility to be creatively
prepared for that request from management. You
can't shift to original production if you have spent
no time building your skill. It doesn't matter how you
open the door to your success, but you do have to
keep in mind what it takes to keep the door open.

As Focus points out,

> If you're talking about a money aspect, if you're
> talking about publishing, then don't sample. A lot
> of people do [overlook the money]. A lot of cats go
> with what feels good; it's not gonna feel good when
> they turn around and want 100 percent of your
> song. It's not gonna feel good when you can't even
> get a percentage of your lyrics because you used so
> much of the sample.

> Everybody needs to get paid—this is our job, this
> is our livelihood—and when you take an old-school
> cat's music and make a new-school song, they want
> new-school money. And a lot of these cats aren't
> getting the budgets, so they can't pay the up-front,
> so they just wind up taking 100 percent of the song.
> "Just give me 100 percent and you're good. You can
> run with it." I wouldn't do it.

On a different note, Hen of Tha Bizness is less concerned about the monetary aspect of the situation
and instead is concerned only with being proficient
and great at whatever one chooses to create:

Just be able to love what you're doing. I don't care, just try to be great. If you wanna be great, just be great at it. Kanye, Just Blaze, Primo, Pete Rock— there's a lot of guys who pioneered sampling and [have] been great at it, provided for their families, made a lot of money, and [have] not had a problem. For us, it doesn't matter, we learned that game, we learned how to sample, we still love doing it, when we feel that vibe ... if that's what we wanna do at a given time, cool.

It's just like working with another producer or collabin' with a cat; it's just like sampling, if you're looking at it from a money approach. You're still gonna have to split the pub[lishing] ... if you're coming up with great music working together, that's just what it is. So, you might as well go ahead and focus on the music and not the money, and try to make the best music possible.

I share Hen's opinion regarding greatness at whatever style you choose to focus on. I also agree that sampling is much like collaborating with another producer (well, except that in this case, your collaborator has the power to take all the publishing). But you have to read deeply into what he said. Hen specified that they learned *that* part of the game. He and Dow spent considerable time learning to master sampling, like every other style of production, because that was their definition of greatness. For Tha Bizness, sampling by itself wasn't enough. They had to know the MPC, they had to know the keyboard, they had to know Southern crunk, West Coast funk,

East Coast boom bap, Midwest bounce. They wanted to be prepared for Top 40 records and pop records. For them, having the ability to lace anyone from Lil Wayne to Chris Brown to the Black Eyed Peas with whatever style they need is essential. For Tha Bizness, that ability goes beyond sampling only. Do you have similar goals? Their philosophy may apply to you.

Regardless of whom I spoke with, everyone's opinion boiled down to the same points: (1) be great at whatever style you choose to employ, and (2) as the ball gets rolling, look at some ways to put yourself in positions to earn maximum income so you can create longevity. Your mindset changes when production is your means to earn a living, send Junior to private school, and put food on the table. Cutting your income with managers and lawyers can be significant enough, but having to slice out another $5-, $10-, or $20K (or far worse) for the owners of that composition and master recording makes a big difference.

What I also want you to take away from this law is that some of the professional producers I've spoken with didn't get snagged creatively when they transitioned from sampling wholly to interpolating or just creating from scratch. They were all talented or resourceful enough to study other disciplines beforehand or learn new ways of creation to keep their careers moving. So keep this in mind as well—this is a process of constant evolution (think Just Blaze going from "U Don't Know" to "Live Your Life" to "Higher" with Baauer).

As REO puts it,

> So, I know people who have done songs that have got on major albums with major artists, no money. No publishing. If you just knew how much that artist was gonna make off that [song], I don't think that you would do it. But again, *it's all relative to what you want.*

Don't suddenly look at your finances with surprise and regret. Understand the advantages and disadvantages of your production weapon of choice. That's what a professional does. That's what a businessman does.

> I was in a particular situation where I happened to flip a sample. I flipped it, and the label loved it, and it was a green light ... all the way to where I got a check. Superstar artist was on it, it was the second single, other superstar artist on the hook, we're about to shoot the video, everything is a go, got it mixed. Like I said, I got paid. I heard people on the phone telling me, "This is gonna be it for you," "This is gonna be a smash," "You're gonna be rich."

> Very, very last minute, they shot the music video, [and] all of a sudden, there's controversy with the sample, and they're asking me now if I can replay what was done. So I did, and at the time, I didn't actually sample the record, I just replayed it myself exactly how it was. So I had another guy come in

and play the guitar, and we did like eight or ten different variations of the riff. The rule was, it's gotta be two notes different, or like some other super-complicated thing.

Either way, I did a bunch of different versions; I did a couple that actually would be equal to what the sample was doing but different enough where we wouldn't have to clear it. But the label came back and said, "No, we like the original one better." Turns out that the people that wanted to clear the sample wanted something absolutely ridiculous, [and at the] end of the day, they didn't want it— the whole entire song was scrapped. And I was like, *"You know what, I would rather just make something original."* —REO of the Soundkillers

People have different opinions on the matter of samples and original production. I don't expect you to agree with my own point of view simply because it's here. Just like you would never pick up a random glass at a bar and guzzle whatever cloudy liquid you find inside, don't gulp down this advice with naïveté. I want you to gather the appropriate information, analyze the situation, and choose your path. The information in this law, as with all of these laws, must align with your vision and make sense for you.

LAW 13

The Winds of Change: Balance Your Sound Against the Market

Producers say they don't listen to the radio. If you don't listen to radio, you shouldn't be in music. I don't care if the same twelve songs are on the radio, you should figure out why those songs are on the radio. —Chuck Greene, 1 Shot Management

OBSERVATION

The sound of popular music changes without fail. It's a guaranteed law of the music industry, no different from the certainty of summer following spring. But when the sound of what's currently popular changes, do you?

In the middle of my grind, I remember the popular sound of the urban sector changing drastically. I studied producers from the era I came up in—Trackmasters, Dr. Dre, Nashiem Myrick, RZA, DJ Premier, Battlecat, Ski, Just Blaze, and Kanye—and I tried to incorporate elements of the '90s and early 2000s in my sound. While I was absorbing these styles and trying to mold one of my own, the wonderful Dipset/Roc-A-Fella/Just Blaze/Kanye West sound of commercial soul emerged in the mainstream. It was the last time I thought I could look to urban radio for inspiration.

You know how you have a warning of only about twenty minutes before a tornado proceeds to rip through your town and lay waste and destruction to all you know and love? That's how the sound of music changed in the mid-2000s. The crunk and snap movement descended upon the South like an evil black cloud, choking the light from my sun-drenched skies. The South was coming into the fold, mangling the sound of popular urban music. Naked, skeleton-esque beats, preschool sounds, meager arrangements, and speaker-blowing 808s were about to dominate the radio. Listening to these beats, I imagined someone recording the sound of babies whacking at the rainbow-colored keys of Fisher-Price pianos, laying drums beneath these rudimentary sounds, and pawning it off as music to the masses. Instantly, the hip-hop production I had known and loved mutated before me.

And I was at the eye of this sonic tornado, smack dab in the middle of the major market in the South, Atlanta, which meant that even being the music snob that I was, I couldn't ignore the change in sound. I wasn't building relationships in New York. I wasn't visiting studios in LA. There was nowhere to run and hide. The situation left me paralyzed; I didn't know how to move. All I knew was that my sample-heavy beat CD was getting two big thumbs down. I was going to have to figure out a way to make it work.

REALIZATION

How do we navigate the differences between the results we want to see from the business, our particular area of ability or gift, and what the market is demanding at the moment? This is a struggle that a lot of producers, new and old, encounter. How do you know? Take a glance around at all the hot producers of the late 1990s and early and mid-2000s whose names are no longer in the credits. The change in popular sound is an unforgiving broom that sweeps hordes of producers into an old, rusty dustpan of obscurity. What will happen when the game changes right in front of you? How will you balance being true to what you're good at, what you enjoy creating, and maintaining a commercial sound if your sound is not commercial? What do you do if you naturally gravitate toward one style but what you do isn't in demand? What do you do if your style doesn't even have a lane yet? How do you navigate your art but keep in sync with what's profitable and commercial? To be you or to be a check-receiver—that is the question. It's a lot to process, and it makes sense to have a game plan, because the last thing you want is to lose your creative mojo and get swept up, too.

There's no easy way to go about answering these questions. I've heard several strategies from a number of producers with ten-plus-year careers. The only way to even approach answering these questions is to be certain of who you are and what your goals are. Sound familiar? That's part of what I warned about in Law 1, Eyes Wide Open, and now you understand the importance of knowing your direction.

Troy Taylor advises,

> If you are having fun doing it, keep doing it, and make it stronger. If you have a quirky sound, if it hits hard, then it's good. If it doesn't hit hard, then it's quirky and bad. You have to make sure that it still fits [and] goes under the auspices of still hitting hard, still sounding good, *still arranged properly, even if it's quirky.*

> A lot of people have a style, they have a sound, and if it doesn't fit and it's not working fast enough for them, then rather than really making sure it fits the format of what's going on, they bend and make it sound like what's going on. I think you can have your own style and fit the format of what's popular. Format can change at any [time]; ... if you change your format, you're maintaining your sound. *If you change your sound and your format to fit what's going on, now you're just becoming a duplicator.* The format is what fits on the radio so that the DJs can fit [it] with their mix and all that stuff. But you keep your sound, your whole thing that makes you smile, that makes you laugh, that makes you stay on the track longer to perfect it. You maintain that.

Troy was writing songs and placing records on Boyz II Men's first album, so I'm certain his perspective on this issue is extremely valuable. Hell, some of you young-'uns may have been conceived to that music. Troy has listened to the sound of R&B morph drastically in the decades he's been making music. He believes, first and foremost, in sticking to the correct format of what's commercially acceptable, a rule you should try not to break regardless of what's going on. If you're trying to sell beats with fifty-second intros and four-bar hooks, you don't want to sell many beats. Also, Troy mentioned the importance of staying true to the elements that make you unique by simply *adjusting* your music to fit what's marketable. Don't give up on yourself, just tweak. The unique perspective that you bring to your music has value, and you don't want to throw that away to become a drone, cloning what's hot at the moment.

To gain more insight, I asked both Needlz and DJ Khalil about this dilemma, and of course (because, like I said, there's no right or wrong way to answer this one), they had opposite responses. Needlz looked at the question from a business point of view: "*You just have to adapt or you die.* I know cats who get stuck with their sound, and they don't wanna change, and there's nobody to shop it to. You gotta change or *update with the times.*" On the other side of the coin, Khalil took more of a creative stance:

I just do me. Pop music is what it is. It's changed since I've been a producer. That's where the faith part comes in; if you continue to do what you do, that sound may very well be the next sound. Anything can become pop. If you're passionate about it, people are gonna hear that passion; [it] doesn't matter what format, what it sounds like. If you have passion and it's unconventional, people are gonna hear that.

They said my music was too backpack. Why [don't I] quantize? Why [does it sound] off? And I just stuck with it. [You] have to believe in what you do. *If it's a good beat, and the song is great, it can be a pop smash.* If it's a moment, it'll live. That's the way you become successful as a producer: you develop a sound, and it eventually becomes pop.

Khalil's process works well for him because of one important factor: he makes amazing music. *If you make inferior music, then you'll be waiting forever for recognition.* His creativity and skill allow him to move this way. To provide you with both sides of the argument, Khalil did drop more jewels of wisdom for us to keep in mind: "You have to pay attention to what's going on. [It's] good to know what's out there, what the *trends* are. A lot of pop music now is manufactured music. A year from now, are you gonna remember [it]?"

While he focuses on the creation of exceptional music and what he does best, he keeps an ear to the ground and isn't blind to what's trending (sometimes to avoid it). With this mix, DJ Khalil has made quite a career of staying true to himself; his clients come to him because they want *his* sound.

Another thing that's massively important is that a lot of what you hear on the radio is horse shit. We all know this—hollow dance and pop songs, repetitive trap music, and the other dreadful trends. I hear things today that make me momentarily envy the deaf. You don't want to abandon what you do to fill a manufactured-music lane that, if you look ahead a few hundred feet, may end abruptly at a cliff.

The production duo Tha Bizness had quite a bit to say on the subject. Hen began with:

> For us, we always adapted to change, and maybe that's because we're from Seattle, and Seattle is so diverse and so accepting of change. Being able to adapt to the way that music changes, we just know that if everybody's on pop music right now, or everybody's on this, we know how to do it our way, but we can also look further. As long as we keep practicing and doing what they want to do, but also doing what we think is gonna be the next shit, then we're always gonna be another step ahead of everybody else.

Dow added,

> We never worry too much about the sound, how's it changing, how it goes. We already know that we're prepared for it, and we always look *to make a true connection with the artist to get the shit done.*

Again, these in-demand producers walk the line between having their own particular spin on things, keeping their creative focus on what they can do to influence the next sound, and knowing what's in demand now. Also at the core of those statements is the fact that, creatively, they're ready for whatever's next, because once again, they've mastered their art. So it doesn't matter what the market throws at them, they're ready to catch it.

By honing his skills, Focus has gained the same level of flexibility:

> I've been fortunate enough to not pigeonhole myself to just hip-hop. When hip-hop made that turn, they started doing the snap and more Southern-sounding beats, I just started working more in R&B, I even did some rock stuff. There's a way that you can integrate it to where you're not selling out. That's what a lot of producers need to learn how to do: keep themselves [skilled] across the board so if something comes up that [they] don't want to deal with, [they can] do something else, [or] try something new.

Focus says he's seen many producers change their sound completely, instead of adjusting, and eventually sell out. There's no need to make such a mistake, because, as he says, "There's a way to integrate what [the industry is] doing at the time and what you're doing at the time."

Blend In Before You Stick Out

Now all of this isn't to say that you can't earn the right to go in a completely different sonic direction while trying to build your unique identity. But it takes time and trust to push a unique sound; it's not something you launch like a pissed-off bull coming out of the gate at a rodeo. On this subject, both DJ Khalil and Dow of Tha Bizness mentioned two great examples: Timbaland and the Neptunes. Dow, well versed in the history of production, elaborated by saying,

> Before you stick out, you have to blend in. You're not necessarily just gonna be the guy out of nowhere; you're not just gonna be the producer guy who just comes with a new sound. Even the most successful producers who came with their own sound, if you listen to their earlier shit, they were just trying to fit in. Like the Neptunes, like Timbo, like some of these cats who changed the sound of radio. In the beginning, they were just trying to get in the door....

> Slowly but surely, they gained people's trust enough to allow ... the artists to feel comfortable enough to try new things with them. It's not gonna just happen overnight. So you gotta understand, if it's your first time working with [an artist], you gotta do what he wants to do. It's not necessarily about you giving him that sound, and you're just gonna be "the guy."

I wanted to include this quote because there may be some of you who have an extremely unique sound and have taken a stance against popular music. I came across these tracks every once in a while as I shopped beats, and I usually knew there wasn't much I could do with them. Some of you cats have the game misunderstood. On the way up, it's highly unlikely that you'll make the industry bend to your will. Observes Chuck Greene,

> We all take the lead from popular [music], but we just add our twist, our original authorship of what's going on. It's hard for you to change time; you have to really climb that scale to make pop music go with you; you have to be on a level of a Dr. Dre with a big machine [behind you].

As a new producer, don't take your sound all the way over the edge and expect every artist you encounter to venture with you into the sonic unknown. Find the right balance between industry conformity and your unique musical identity. As you progress, bring more of that uniqueness into the fold. What you don't want is to become so rigid and locked into the belief that as a newbie producer, you're going to automatically change the game with a radical sound. That's highly improbable.

THE FINAL MIX

Do you even have a sound to be concerned about? Perhaps you haven't found your niche yet, and you're just composing whatever comes to heart. That's fine, too. Some of us don't build a unique identity. We just make music. If that's the case, just seek greatness.

Personally, I lucked out, because something good did blossom out of an otherwise dismal situation. While I was losing out on the snap and crunk, I luckily ran into another shift in popular music that was both something I liked and something that would allow me to maintain who I was. The Jeezy sound (first-generation trap)—trumpet blaring, baritone-sax-fueled street anthems advanced forward with chunky 808s, and rapid 1/32 hi-hats—evolved and surfaced in mainstream hip-hop. Once his sound became prevalent, and I got to experience these huge records with gritty epic beats, I found a new lane that not only sounded promising to me, but also forced me off the MPC and into Reason to try to create from scratch.

Regardless of what's going on, creative mastery is the first piece of the puzzle, essential to either producing music that incorporates the current trends or becoming adept at your own style. Develop the musical elements that make you unique, keeping one ear on what's going on now and the other ear on what the future sound might be. If you have a style, don't abandon it. If you don't have a style, maybe it's on the way, and if it's not, just focus on making the best music you can.

As Chuck Greene advises, "You have to stay in the realm of what's going on. What are these companies investing their money in?" If you plan to make a living doing this, create your best work and keep it in the realm of what's marketable. If you don't care about a check and you're going to do you, then forget about what's popular. Be a monster at what you do best. You may or may not break the bank, but you're okay with that because you're moving how you want to move. *Be honest with yourself and make sure your actions are in alignment with your goals.*

> I think that as much as we creative people want to feel like [we] can do whatever we want, there definitely has to be a business plan and some sort of insight about what kind of ideas are being sold. We're in the business of selling music, so, just like any other sort of business, you have to cater to your audience.

> Once a certain genre of music really starts taking over the radio, the A&Rs want more of that. I'm a big ballad guy, a lot of people know me because of different ballad stuff I've done. And for a while there, people really liked that. And all of a sudden, right when I was getting that going, Top 40 radio started speeding up and turning into 120 BPMs, 127, and my ballads [weren't] what people wanted anymore. The slower ballad-type songs I had on hold were being released back to me because they weren't "relevant" anymore. All of it dropped. People's albums were getting re-A&Re'd and everything. So, of course, I had to get on that and learn how to make that music and research [it]. I [was] already a fan of dance music, but you know, I really had to do the research and know what sounds

to use and what sounds not to use, this and that. Being a businessman means you have to keep up with the trends of the industry you are in. So it definitely changed my perspective business-wise, but also creatively. —REO

Part 4: What Should I Be Doing?

LAW 14

Out of Time: Take Command of Your Most Precious Asset

I could sit in the studio all day long; it's like a paradise to me.
—Focus

OBSERVATION

"Time," by Pink Floyd, is one of my favorite songs on this planet. The song is a seven-minute sonic adventure that explores the nature of time's passage, the ill use of our most precious resource, and the mediocrity left in its wake. This song is a perfect mental soundtrack for the discussion at hand.

Way back, while living in Atlanta, I reluctantly helped a friend move. Another friend of ours helping with the move was a novice beatmaker. Our mutual friend was telling the newbie beatmaker how he'd witnessed me critiquing the beats of another producer. Upon hearing that I was a person with production knowledge, he enthusiastically offered to play me some songs. Point number one. He enthusiastically offered to play songs. *Not beats*. *Songs*. (Also note that he jumped without hesitation to play music for someone who may have been able to help him, despite the fact that I looked exhausted and my eyeballs were darting around as I planned my escape.)

As I was listening to his production, I had to ask him several times how long he had been producing. This aspiring producer had been making music for approximately one and a half years, and he was pretty damn good. The mixes needed work, and his sound selection needed some evolution, but from a composition and construction point of view, he was unexpectedly dope. *Time.* He reminded me of athletes who pick up a new sport, and because they're athletic as hell, they're out there viciously dunking on people and whacking fast balls beyond the fence, unlike the non-athlete who has to practice harder to make up for the lack of natural ability.

REALIZATION

So after suppressing my initial jealousy of this cat who didn't play a lick of piano and yet was banging out chord progressions like some sort of savant, I refocused on the material and some of the other positives of the lesson. In this short period of *time* (you already know that a year and a half is nothing but a drop in the bucket for us), this cat had *full songs* for his tracks. *He did not play me a beat CD. He did not play instrumentals.* He had songs and explained the vision for each song he played for me.

Furthermore, the newbie was already paired with a talented MC who seemed to be a strong match for his production. This pairing further enhanced the beauty of what he was doing. And lastly, he was telling me that he was in the process of shopping a song to the strip club DJs in Atlanta, the record-breakers of the South (the song was pretty damn good, too). So wait, let me get this straight: you started making beats, you got pretty good, you found artists to work with, and you're already shopping records, all without any direction?

I hope all of you recognize this gentleman's gangster. I went four years and made *none* of these excellent moves, and here was this producer, a year and a half in, with full songs, rapped and sung over, and he was already taking records to the tastemakers in his market. Pure genius! He was working with his own artists, learning what it took to produce not just tracks but full songs. The processes were inseparable for him. These are moves that take some producers years to realize and then make.

This newbie producer was attempting to skip straight over beatmaker status and was doing his best to move toward becoming a producer. There wasn't a laundry list of excuses—no "Well, I'm looking for a songwriter" or "I don't have anywhere to record so I didn't put anything down on this" or "Well, here's the instrumental, and I got this vision for it, let me explain it to you while you walk to your car." There was no library full of half-finished beats—none of that. The vocals on one of his tracks were a little muddy, so he informed me that just to get the song completed, he had recorded vocals on his Guitar Hero mic. You're going to record on a Guitar Hero mic just to get it done? Are you serious?

Life gives us beautiful lessons if we only take the time to look and stay focused and present enough to see them. If you're an aspiring producer, please take note of the usage of your time. There are people accomplishing in one or two years what took me four. There are people accomplishing twice as much in half the time because of their attitudes and vision, which influence their actions and what they do with their time, day by day. Just sitting on a bunch of beat CDs wasn't even in the program for this cat. He went in an entirely different direction. In addition to learning and doing so much in such a short period of time, he had the vision to see what a producer was. He leapfrogged over the typical steps and saved himself months, maybe even years. I'm sure he didn't realize all of this, but I did, and I was glad I could see it. Now you can see it.

The Minutes, Hours, Days and Weeks:

I want to focus now on how the minutes, hours, days, and weeks factor into your success as a producer.

After you've absorbed this example, let me ask you, what are you doing with your time? Have you been producing for three, five, six, eight years and have yet to make your own brand-building and career-growing moves? Again, this is cold water in the face, a smack across the cheek. Are you wasting time being a one-dimensional beatmaker in your room?

Time is one of the most important aspects of production success. Talent is a major factor, desire is a major factor, skill is a major factor—but without time to dedicate to mastering and hustling beats, you have nothing. It's sad to admit, but there are producers out there who can win or earn significantly higher levels of success than you simply because they have more time to put into production, not because of their talent.

If you're working a corporate gig, sitting in traffic, getting to the gym, spending an hour with your family, and then getting to music from 9 or 10 p.m. until 2 a.m., or getting to the studio only to get back home at 1 a.m. so you can get adequate rest before work the next day, you're in a totally different situation than a college student or someone who doesn't even have a job. It's unfortunate that both of these types of producers could have equal levels of potential, equal levels of talent, but one simply has more time to either work on his tracks, shop them, or sit in the studio with artists till the sun comes up. People in the music industry are vampires—they're nocturnal, getting it in while everyone else sleeps. If you can't be in the studio at 4:30 in the morning when an artist is in his or her creative zone, and someone else can, success boils down to a function of time.

Always keep time in mind when you're creating. If you want this, you may have to rearrange your life to devote an adequate amount of time to the craft. That rearrangement could come in the form of a job that's less demanding (and yes, earning less money), maybe a different shift, or a different career altogether. It could come from changing your commute, scaling back at the gym, scaling back on sleep, or even worse, scaling back on your family time. Trust and believe, the people who are giving advice in this book have all scaled back on time with their families, and some of them are haunted by regret for willingly paying such a high cost. Troy Taylor mentioned that he wished he'd trusted in God's path for him and hadn't spent his time worrying about keeping his career afloat, thus working extra hard and losing precious time he could've invested in his son. But the truth is, most successful producers are true workaholics, out of both passion and necessity. Focus tells us,

> One of the wonderful things about working with Aftermath and Dre ... was we had studios at our disposal. So, Dre would just put us in there, and we would make our own hours. So I would literally go

in at about one-thirty, two, every day and leave at about five, six, maybe seven o'clock the next day, and that's how we ran our regimen.

Never underestimate the daily commitment required. Way back, when she thought I was slacking, Felisha Booker, the founder and CEO of Dynamic Producer and my former boss, liked to jab me with a reminder that we only get twenty-four hours. She would ask me, "What are you doing with every waking hour of your day?" What are you doing with yours?

THE FINAL MIX

Time runs out on a dope producer every day. Life, responsibilities, finances, family, and/or business can suddenly grab hold of a producer who can out-produce the general-producer population and grind him to a screeching halt. Like a hitman, circumstances step in and unapologetically and coldly murder your ability to give it your all. That overburdened producer throws his hands up in the air, hangs his head low, and suddenly realizes that he doesn't have the time to go hard at his dream of waking up every morning to walk over to the studio and make music for a living. *That producer now realizes he's only got time for a hobby.*

If this book is any indication of how much I love music producers, then you know it's depressing for me to even type that paragraph. Remember what I said earlier: it's more difficult to get things popping when life is in your face demanding its just due. Not impossible, but more difficult. Please maximize your time. Do not waste your minutes, hours, or days in this journey. They all add up. What are you doing on a daily basis? How is your time spent creating? Are you being effective? Focused, purposeful, daily action is key to winning as a producer.

If you're like I was, sitting there with a library full of beats and no songs, take more control of your own destiny. Shift your time toward building your own brand with an artist—pop, urban, dance, whatever it is you do. Instead of being repetitive, sitting and waiting for someone to create your future for you, take the time to broaden the horizons of your production.

I end this chapter by offering you insight from wise Jedi Master Chuck Greene on how one needs to maximize one's time. It would make sense that some of the best information I heard regarding time management would come from a manager, one who's responsible for making sure a certain amount of output is produced in a certain amount of time. Chuck informed me that,

> A lot of people can't work for themselves; they need someone above them telling them to be at work at eight, take their first break at ten, second at twelve o'clock, out at four or five. They need that structure

and order given from someone else. You go to your room and you work at the studio *when you want to,* and you work as hard as *you want to.* Whether you go in your room and watch SportsCenter or work on your craft is on you. A lot of people are just not self-motivated and don't understand [that] you have to work without somebody telling you this is what you have to do. You don't have a boss in your room.

Remember, you're both the manager and the employee. Have you been letting yourself off the hook? Chuck continued,

[It's about] having accountability for your workload. If you work a factory job—[let's say] paper—[there's] a quota for how much paper has to come out a week ... same thing for beats. [There] has to be a quota set, and you gotta try your best weekly to meet your quota. You've gotta set some parameters.... "I'm gonna do X-Y-Z this week," [and you've] gotta stick to it and do it. If not, you're gonna get caught up in the cycle.

The average guy can go through forty, fifty, sixty tracks before something sticks. If you've got twenty dope tracks in your catalogue, your chances are slim. You have to manage your creative output. This is work, chief. Clock in, clock out.

Furthermore, when you get in that room for your daily shift, employ maximum focus. This law isn't just about dedicating the appropriate amount of time; it's also about using that time efficiently. Troy says,

Whenever I decide to make music, *I make it, I do it, I start it, I finish it.* Whatever I don't finish, I just get off it and come back to it. But ... whatever I start, I get into it. Whatever I put my mind to, I stay with it. I don't have a schizophrenic creative vibe. Most kids have that because they have an ADD creative pattern—talking, texting, and then they end up not finishing, not staying focused on what it is they started.

Ours is the era of infinite distraction. If I walked into your home, unplugged your television, and strolled out with it on my back, you'd be pretty pissed. You don't like the notion of someone stealing your television, do you? Then why be comfortable with someone or something stealing your time? You can buy another damn television. Time is the one thing we can't get back. There are devices all around you that provide a million clever ways to steal your precious time. As a producer, you must be above the activities that waste the time of the ordinary. Your line of work does not give you the luxury. Avoid these crafty thieves—your YouTube videos, and Instagram, and your Vines, and your apps with cool games, and your Twitter, and your reality TV. There is a time for these things. You're not a machine: you need to have fun. But when you work, work. Focus intently on your craft.

One last message geared toward those of you who'll receive this book early on in your journey. Earlier in the book, I discussed the importance of starting immediately. Not only should you start now if you've been thinking about it, but if possible, *start early*. As I learn of new producers rising in popularity, more and more often I find myself running across producers who are able to gain significant traction at a young age. But these aren't overnight success stories. Many of these young producers are catching the bug early—playing in the church band, taking music lessons, or experimenting with production as children.

Think about the advantage of learning about theory, production, and DAWs at such an early age. If you started at fifteen and were able to gain some placements at twenty-two, that's eight years of skill developed to allow those achievements. The guy who's twenty-three and started at fifteen is in the same sonic boat as the guy who's thirty yet started at twenty-two. But at thirty, you're moving toward carrying a world of responsibility on your shoulders. That young guy is fresh out of college and has much more maneuvering room.

Many of the professionals I've spoken with were well into a high level of skill during college and able to skip past getting a "real" job because they were good enough to earn placements directly out of or during college. Timing makes a big difference to someone who's chasing a dream, and production is no different. Of course, success can come at any time,

but I'm telling you what I've learned from the producers I've spoken with. I want you to recognize the
blessings of youth and freedom and make sure you
don't squander those blessings. The earlier, the easier.
Music production is already challenging enough, and
you want to take advantage of *anything* that will give
you an edge.

LAW 15

One in a Million: Avoid Becoming Discouraged by the Competition

What's gonna separate you from the next person nowadays? Everybody has the same amount of tools; there's no excuse now. —DJ Khalil

OBSERVATION

Parents may love their child deeply, but it benefits them to be able to objectively see that despite their love and guidance, their child may be terrible with decisions, spoiled, irresponsible, or just a jerk. I try to assess the production community with the objective eyes of a mindful parent. And my objective eyes reveal an unfortunate truth: many "lost" beatmakers with little respect for the game have crept up on the music industry like roaches. The technological and social barriers to entry have been removed, and from under the stove of mediocrity, an infestation of wannabe beatmakers has swarmed the production kitchen, clicking mindlessly at their software and hammering away at their midi drum machines. Some of these roaches are doing music for some perceived fame, for fat bank accounts, to have groupies hanging off of them like Christmas-tree ornaments, or to strap on shiny watches whose makers' names they can't properly pronounce. A generation of music creators has been brainwashed by the perceived success of the music business and they want their damn piece of the entertainment industry pie.

I may sound harsh, but if you're in this game to make mediocre music for a check, then to me, you're a production roach. On the other hand, I love the people who dedicate themselves to mastering production. I love how they approach it, what they're willing to put themselves through to achieve it. I have little respect for those who run contrary to that dedication, that level of respect for this art, crawling all over something they don't fully respect and appreciate. As Needlz says,

> *This is not easy.* I'm not sure if you're doing this because you love music or the money. If it's for the money, nine times out of ten, *you're gonna be wack.* You're gonna make the same beat over and over to get the money.

If you're not doing this for true love, I beg you to re-examine your motives and approach this form of expression as an art and craft you devote yourself entirely to. There are people who live for the creation of music. Focus is one of them:

> I've never had a passion for something so much in my life. Never ever. There was nothing else that told me this is what I was supposed to do. I made

my first song when I was six on the piano. It was a stupid song; it was literally less than a minute long, and it was called, "Everybody Loves Me." But I knew from six until my current age, there was nothing else that gave me the drive to have the passion to go out and do it by all and any means necessary. I had no choice. I had no damn choice.

REALIZATION

I remember sitting in my living room years ago, in a negative mood as I thought about the infestation, the ballooning number of producers in the market, and what this meant for the business. A surplus of providers means that their products become commodities, and in music, this means that everyone has a harder time surviving as a result. As I relayed my crap thinking to a producer-friend of mine, he ended up sharing some positive wisdom with me that I would like to share with you—wisdom that I hope will support you as you contemplate the sheer volume of competitors in your market.

We talked about the explosion of beatmakers onto the production world and what this meant for aspiring producers. He agreed with me that the ridiculous influx of new beatmakers has spawned overwhelming odds and competition. He also agreed that the odds of beatmakers getting checks and thriving as bona fide producers have diminished substantially. But unlike me, he held a positive point of view that I now pass along to you: the more people trying to achieve the same dream, the better it looks when the blood, sweat, and tears you've poured into excelling beyond the pack make it glaringly obvious that *you are exceptional.* And all those poor souls standing behind you like you were the Verizon man have served to make you look magnificent.

Let me paint a picture so you can visualize the current situation. Imagine a magnificent galaxy painted with colorful dust and clouds and thousands of gleaming stars burning off crazy amounts of energy as they illuminate the darkness. See, there are billions of stars within this galaxy, but only a few burn so hot and are so intense that they stand out enough to be seen clearly in the darkest night sky. They are twinkling jewels projecting brilliance greater than their counterparts within the galaxy.

The fact that you know there are a billion stars in that galaxy but you can see only a few reminds you of how impressive those few are. You must become one of these clearly visible stars. Today, you've got to burn so brightly with talent and skill that your light is obvious and undeniable. You must be consistently amazing. The people in the business aren't stupid. A&Rs, artists, and managers know what's out there. They know how good you have to be to set yourself apart from the pack. They know that the bar has been raised to the clouds. Your heat must be irrefutable. To build a career, you must be the brightest, hottest star among the millions behind you, and by relentlessly pounding on your craft, you can be.

So what are you going to do about this? You have a choice, as with anything in life. Once you recognize that there are billions of other stars in this galaxy, you can burn the light of mediocrity or you can have the correct conversation with yourself. As you read this law, aware of your own power, you should think, "If there are mad producers out there fighting for the same piece of glory, my only opportunity for success lies in building incredible skill, skill that *must* make me stand out from everyone else, *amateur or professional.*" Here's where the upcoming chapter on excellence reveals its importance. If this is what you want, if this is what you dream about when your eyelids close at night, if this is what you see and nothing else, you must practice a code of excellence.

THE FINAL MIX

Sometimes the way that we're able to view a problem helps us find our way through it. Production is terribly crowded. I hope I've given you a way to view the situation that helps you keep your mind off of the problem and on your craft instead, on how you're going to set yourself apart from the crowd.

Some of you will have to make tough decisions and figure out how to find the time, funds, and heart to burn as brightly as possible so that when that A&R, manager, or close friend of the artist goes through his daily hundred or so tracks and songs via e-mail, yours is the hottest, and all of a sudden all the dim stars behind you just made you look damn good. The only way to win and keep winning in today's game is to be both exceptionally creative and exceptionally prolific. Hen said it best when he explained to me, "To try to find success in this business, shit's getting cheaper and shit's getting easier to produce, and you can do whatever you want to make hits nowadays." The playing field is level. You may have gotten away with being pretty good several years ago, but now, to stand out from the crowd, you have to be amazing!

Use the odds against you as motivation to succeed. Shine brightly.

LAW 16

Par Excellence: Employ Creative and Mental Techniques to Master Your Craft

Do you think about having a legacy? —Needlz

OBSERVATION

To stand out from the pack, you understand that there's no other option than being incredible. You'll need to inspire people to become crazy over your work. They should ask about you in the comments section of YouTube videos. You want them furiously Googling the instrumental versions of your work. Managers and A&Rs should be in an uproar, verbally sawing their staffs in half for not having *you* on their radars. Before the manhunt can commence, before fans are on Twitter confessing their undying love for your music, you must first develop your talents and then incessantly hammer on them with exceptional skill. You must ascend to the level of undeniability and the consistent screwface. Seeking and obtaining excellence accomplishes this.

The mindset of striving for excellence applies to any worthy life aspiration. My father said to me when I was a kid, "Son, even if you shovel chicken shit for a living, you had better be the best damn chicken-shit shoveler there ever was." Regardless of what you end up doing, you do it to the best of your ability. This kind of thinking is so important because many people have grown accustomed to mediocrity. You see mediocrity on the streets, walking to a job it hates in the morning. It's in the Honda Civic in the next lane when you're sitting in traffic. Mediocrity is asking you what kind of cheese you want on your sandwich and standing behind you reading *People* magazine in the checkout line at Walgreens. You, my friend, will vehemently deny mediocrity. As mediocrity is shunned, you will instead commit to achieving excellence, seeking to continuously use your music to drop people's jaws until the drool dribbles onto their collars.

As we discussed, the more people there are in your industry trying to squeeze through the same narrow door, the better you must be. Average producers remain at the front gate. Pretty good producers get to hang out on the lawn. Hot but inconsistent producers actually get to knock. The producers who abide by excellence, who did what they had to day after day, who supplemented their talent by relentlessly beating on their craft, they put their foot through the door until it comes flying off the damn hinges. Then they stroll right through. The majority of their music is of extremely high quality and the beatmaking God readily welcomes them with a comfortable seat inside the Kingdom of Producer Success.

You're thinking to yourself, "Yea, I got it, excellence, excellence, excellence. Check." The question now is, how is excellence achieved? What's the curriculum of course work that leads to screwed faces, to heads nodding furiously until they're on the verge of snapping loose from their necks and rolling away? What follows is a syllabus of production strategies that will last you for years. Below is a series of habits, techniques, and mindsets that will be your whetstone. By adopting all that follows in this chapter, you'll grind your blade of skill until you are idolized by the young producers behind you, until the competition becomes frantic when they learn they're up against you for a record, until you're a musical force to be reckoned with.

You'll learn the tenets of production excellence from those who have used them to build their own beautiful careers, combined with some examples of my breaking those rules as pitfalls to avoid. By the end of this chapter, the motivation will pulsate in your chest, and you'll feel like you're strapped into the seat of a rocket, listening to the countdown, waiting to launch to the next stages of your creativity. Shall we begin?

Be Obsessed With Greatness

I tried to make a commitment to being great for two reasons. First, I was completely strung out on the feeling I got when someone told me they loved one of my beats. I've never experienced the feeling of shooting heroin or done a line of cocaine, but that would be my guess for the right analogy to describe the pure electric, surging wave of ecstasy that fired through me when I took someone where they needed to go with music and gave them the screwface. What a beautifully addictive feeling. Second, out of sheer competition, I wanted to be better than everybody else. That inner flame kept me sitting in front of my computer hour after hour, day after day, with the specific goal of improving (but under my own terms, unfortunately).

I remember working so hard that I'd have to pee, and I would hold it, dancing at my MPC until my bladder was giving me the middle finger. I couldn't leave; I had to get it right. I would stumble around the keyboard trying to find what key my sample was in or what chord was in my head, and I would get so frustrated I'd give myself a headache.

However, despite the MPC dancing, while I was writing this book it became obvious that even though I *thought* I'd been working toward greatness, it wasn't enough. There are different levels of commitment to greatness. There's a vast difference between saying to yourself, "I am committed to *this* purpose" and setting the boat ablaze so there's no retreat. There was more that I should have been doing on a daily basis, more time I should have been spending to cultivate real greatness. Your own quest for greatness should keep you dancing in your studio, too. But as you progress, I urge you to avoid my mistake and make sure that your quest for greatness is genuine.

> It comes down to the mind state. The reason we have a catalog worth so much and have a quantity of so much quality is because we knew we wanted to be great. —Dow, Tha Bizness

Everything begins with the mind, the heart, and the thought process. *Your mind is the strongest piece of equipment you have in the studio. When you have proper command of that tool, everything else at your disposal becomes a true weapon.* Early on, Tha Bizness knew that greatness was the *only* option; their focus on true greatness is embedded within every action taken and decision made. DJ Khalil is no different:

> You shouldn't be doing this if you're not trying to achieve a certain form of excellence, literally. I guess it is a choice, but it should be *every day*, a part of who you are, period.

Every day. A part of who you are. Is it a part of you? Here's Troy Taylor's take:

That's with anything I do, I gotta be the best at it. Just the quality of what I do has to be perfect. Even if it's trendy, grimy, or whatever, it still has to be perfect within that realm.

Another Platinum-plus producer fueled by the desire to be the best. Noticing a trend here? It doesn't matter what style of music you're working on, it has to be "perfect within that realm." Greatness. Excellence. The best. Over and over again!

Focus recalls,

It was almost a mantra. I used to get up every day and tell myself that I was striving to be *legendary*. So, I surpassed excellence; I surpassed greatness; I wanted to go to legendary. To get to the place where Quincy Jones is sitting, and Russ Titelman and David Foster and real producers that I looked up [to] and still look up to [to] this day.

Focus shot right past greatness to legendary. What are you waking up and telling yourself first thing in the morning?

Studying

Earlier on, we took up different styles of production like they were martial arts and practiced to gain our belts. Like that's just how I look at it. Like doing ballads to doing R&B to doing every style of hip-hop, from West Coast [to] Southern music to how they had the swing in the Midwest to how they had the hardcore boom bap in the East to even having the sampled commercial sound of the late

'90s to being able to do the stuff that sounded like Southern drums in '98 versus Southern drums in 2010. We learned it, we studied it, we practiced it over and over again 'til the point where it became a black belt in ballads, a black belt in Southern music, a black belt in whatever we were doing. — Dow, Tha Bizness

Dow's quote illustrates beautifully a vivid picture of commitment. This is a technique I don't hear often, and I know that I didn't implement this approach in my production. Tha Bizness broke down different disciplines of production, dissecting the elements behind each of them, training themselves to be proficient in various genres and markets around the country. That's an extraordinary study strategy and years of dedication, persistence, and work. I, on the other hand, was an East Coast/sample man all day. I knew nothing about an R&B track, a ballad, pop, or Midwest bounce. Occasionally, I experimented with a West Coast vibe or a Southern feel, but I wasn't proficient. This technique of mastering disciplines requires a serious level of dedication to excellence. I wasn't ready for that level of commitment. But look where that commitment has taken Tha Bizness.

Why [does] this sound like this? [I] really studied cats—Primo, Havoc, Pete Rock. At first, I sounded like them, but after a year and a half, two years, I came up with my own style, [a] kind of hybrid of all my influences. Study the greats, work hard, [and] listen…. —Needlz

Needlz, among a few other cats, stresses the importance of knowing the history of the greats, understanding their music, and studying their techniques. In his quote, he brought up something that DJ Khalil also mentioned: emulation. In an effort to improve, they emulated the greats, eventually merging their own styles with what they'd learned from legends.

Be infinitely curious. Listen deeply and understand how Timbaland is able to maintain such a signature sound, despite making hits in multiple genres for two decades. Why does it seem like the Neptunes' tracks have the simplest of melodies, yet they're so powerfully addictive? Know Just Blaze, study the Runners, and discover why their tracks have so much energy and what Just is doing to flip samples in such a unique way. Break down the underrated genius of Mannie Fresh; understand why he was the production foundation of one of the most successful record label regimes in hip-hop. Comprehend the skill behind Stargate; figure out what it is about their music that allowed them to come from Scandinavia and become monsters in the U.S. while producers who live here can't make moves. Understand how the J.U.S.T.I.C.E. League has completely revolutionized the way people sample and has raised the interpolation bar so high you need a fireman's ladder to get to it. They're so damn good that even as a sample junky, I listen to their music and I can't even map out the architecture of where the sample ends and original music begins. Ask yourself: "How did they get that to sound like that?" "Why was this song so catchy?" "How can they recycle their sounds, yet the beats sound so fresh?" "Is that in the sample or did they replay that?"

I studied a few producers pretty intensely, not necessarily with the purpose of seeking greatness but out of curiosity, which ended up serving me well. If the sample tended to be a loop, that was pretty obvious: the skill came from finding the rare sample and putting dope drums to it. But there were some records that were more complex, and I had to know how they were born.

I remember attempting to re-create three beats in particular. The first was "You Know My Steez" by Gang Starr. I found the Joe Simon sample and threw the section I thought I heard into the MPC. After a little time playing with notes, I re-created DJ Premier's legendary groove. It was like discovering treasure; it opened my mind to a whole new way of sampling. Until then, I was grabbing huge loops, not taking into account the level of creative freedom you give yourself when you break the sample down to notes.

The second beat I remember working on was Ghostface's "One," produced by JuJu of the Beatnuts. It was a loop, but I was intrigued by the sinister sound of the piano progression, and I squealed like a toddler on Christmas morning when I finally got my hands on the sample. What drove me nuts was that as I kept searching through the sample, I couldn't find the exact section that JuJu had sampled from; the only thing that came close had a guitar melody dancing through it. I threw the sample in a wave editor and realized that the left and right channels had different-looking waveforms. I isolated one and noticed that the guitar was in only one channel. JuJu cut out the side with the guitar and doubled the side with the keys (or made it mono), thus amplifying the sample and bringing life to that grimy piano progression. It blew my mind because I wouldn't have thought of going that deep to get what I wanted from the beat. But now I knew.

The third one I remember trying to re-create came from Kanye's production on Shyne's *Godfather Buried Alive* album. He produced a track entitled "More or Less," which sampled the song "Rose" by Lamont Dozier. I had the vinyl that contained that sample, so I knew it immediately when I heard what Kanye did. What I couldn't understand was where he was getting these extra notes. I went back, mimicking Kanye's chops until I realized that he was cutting in between notes, adjusting the attack, and then hitting the same note again to extend it. The attack was set so perfectly, and the volume of the second note was diminished as if to make it sound like the first note was sustained and dropped off in volume naturally. He was essentially manipulating the sample so it sounded like it lasted for a full quarter-beat. That level of chopping precision enlightened me about the power at your fingertips when you've mastered those chops. By studying and attempting to re-create what I was hearing, I opened the door to new ways of creating and quickly began incorporating what I had learned into my sample-based production.

> Study the greats and develop your own sound. Know Premier, Pete Rock, 45 King, Rick Rubin. Know The Bomb Squad. Know the history of the producers and records—Large Pro, J Dilla. Study the greats. You have to mimic them in a way to actually get to a point where you have your own sound. All of a sudden you're like, "Damn, I have my own sound." That's how you become good. Even Kobe had to study Jordan to become great. Study the greats in order to become great, period. —DJ Khalil

Wise words from one of the most creative producers of the twenty-first century.

> I think, first and foremost, they need to really choose what [it] is that they want to be. If they say, ... "I really wanna be a good producer," [there are] some things you can do at home, [with] no money. Go through your catalog of music in your iTunes and listen to all the things that work—successful [or] highly successful. Analyze them; listen to

them. Figure out why, whether you like it or not, figure out why it was successful. Go through the things that came out and didn't do well. Analyze them, listen to them, really pick them apart. Figure out why. —Troy Taylor

This was something I never learned to do until I was delivering beats from Dynamic Producer members to labels and artists. As the person delivering the music, I had to suddenly start listening to hits to understand why certain songs got heavy rotation on the radio and in the clubs. Only then would I be adept at picking the correct beats to pass along. As a producer, I never stopped to analyze why some things on the radio worked and why some things didn't. I can tell you that you'll give yourself a strong advantage by having in-depth insight into what kinds of records work and become successful. Look deeply into the nature of arrangements, progressions, melodies, drums, and lyrics. Troy gives some excellent advice. Be sure to make it a part of your arsenal.

Creative Versatility, Preparation, and Patience

A lot of cats were surprised to see all the R&B joints we were doing. They were like, "Damn, I thought y'all just did rap beats...." But we were like, "No, we've just been waiting for an opportunity." Now that we've had this opportunity with R. Kelly, T-Pain, Chris Brown, or whatever, ... now we're able to get heard ... and that's all it's about. It's about being ready. So we can sit there and play

the beats for whoever. It might be Chris Brown, and he's loving the ballads. Then go into the next room and chill with Busta, and he wants the super-wild sound. And then into the next room and be with Drake and Wayne and they want some soft, melodic, R&B hard shit or whatever.... It's just ... being prepared and ... having that catalog ready.
—Dow, Tha Bizness

What's dope about Tha Bizness is that because of their desire for greatness, they've preemptively trained in each discipline, and they're prepared for any opportunity. They walked through the doors that rap opened and ran right into R&B and pop. Their work ethic, those hours/days/weeks/months/years of preparation, puts Tha Bizness in a position where they're simply ready for any phone call. This is how you attain longevity. If one genre is slow, they're not stuck; they can change direction at any time. Without a doubt, these are exceptional producers.

Peep what Focus had to add about developing versatility:

Even Dre is a legendary producer, and he's still living. Stevie is an incredible, legendary producer and somebody I still look up to immensely. Prince—I wanna be like that. So every day I used to get up and tell myself, what are you gonna do that's gonna top what you did yesterday? What are you gonna do that's gonna set the trend for next year? How are you gonna turn around and stay relevant?

Now, if you turn around and pigeonhole yourself into a style, then you will not be relevant. Back when I was coming up in the grind, you had a year and a half, almost two years with a sound. Now it's six months. That's it, you got a six-month window. If you don't hit, you gotta change your sound after six months. So, I had to keep myself on that grind. Five a day. Five beats a day, I'm gonna turn around and reinvent myself, *make sure none of those five sound like the five I did yesterday.* —Focus

What an incredible recipe for versatility and preparation. Following this strategy requires a lot of discipline. Pushing out five beats a day is already hard enough. But five beats that don't sound like the beats you made yesterday? If you can handle such a training regimen, you'll be a freak of versatility, a creator who can spread his signature sound through a variety of styles.

Dow shared some excellent advice about preparation as it relates to prolificacy and longevity:

One of the main things is just preparing yourself for your success. One of the major things that's always helped us out was, the catalog's there. So a lot of cats will get that one record to pop, and then *they haven't really been studying their craft as much* and don't have that many beats that are cool on deck. Once you hit and they quote you as the "it" guy, you gotta keep coming with it because *everybody and their mama's gonna ask you,* "Yo, I want that *same* sound, *same* beat, gimme *that*...." And if you don't got it, it's gonna be over for you!

Just like you've seen with a whole bunch of producers, they were the hot guys for six months, and then that journey was over! That's what's been one of our biggest keys to success; … we've got a couple thousand beats just ready, [and] we're always making new ones. But having that catalog just helps out. —Dow, Tha Bizness

Dow's forthright quote stings—it's the equivalent of hitting your pinky toe on the leg of a very sturdy chair. How many times have we seen the new "it" guy get hot for six months and then disappear into oblivion? "Hey, what happened to so and so?" This is a twofold process—you have to fight, claw, and scratch to get in the building, and then you have to hold on for dear life to stay. Many of you are already pretty damn talented. But are you prolific enough to continuously bring the fire?

I was the prime example of this mistake. I had a couple of nice joints on the beat CD, but it was false advertising because there was no catalog behind it. I couldn't sit there and run through fifty to sixty beats of heat in one listening session, and that's what it takes. A couple of thousand beats? Damn!

[It's about] preparation and hard work. Being willing to learn. Understand that it's a long process. [It] doesn't happen overnight. [Patience] comes with the territory [and success] depends on how badly you want it and how much pride you take in your work. —DJ Khalil

Patience! I was awful. I had no patience. I had to be nice, *now!* I used to get so frustrated because I wanted to progress at a pace that doesn't exist for many. That frustration strangled me mentally, and instead of focusing on daily work and evolution, I was busy pouting, my arms crossed like a ten-year-old brat, because I wasn't better than I was. Four years honing my skills and mastering my craft was absolutely nothing to complain about. I didn't have the right to be frustrated and whine, because I now know that the producers that I looked up to were doing the same drills *daily* for seven, ten, twelve years to master their sound. This dream takes time—lots and lots of it. With time, you're also going to need patience.

Benchmarking

> If you wanna get your sound on the radio, and you play your stuff and it doesn't sound anywhere close to what people are doing on the radio, but you just truly believe that your shit is *the* shit, maybe you can just continue to believe that until something magically happens for you, or you can continue to benchmark yourself against others.... Say, "Okay, what am I doing wrong?" or "How can I make myself better?" or "How can I compete in this climate?" —Dow, Tha Bizness

Benchmarking. I don't think I heard another word out of Dow and Hen's mouths more than "bench-

marking." The duo is adamant about knowing where
they stand. Remember the producer's sound-deprivation box? That doesn't exist for Tha Bizness. Dow
explained, "That's the main thing that some people
just don't do. They'll just think they're the hottest
shit out, but they haven't listened and compared
themselves to what's winning, compared themselves
to some of their idols." They know this is a competition—you're fighting for every opportunity in this
game—and Dow and Hen constantly compare themselves to the best. I don't think a lot of producers
understand that when you're sending their music all
around the country to various companies, individuals, managers, and coordinators, you're competing
with the Neptunes. Mr. A&R just got finished running through Rob Knox's music, and you're next.
Everybody's trying to land work on that one album.
Know where you stand, know where you need to improve, know where you need to evolve. You do this by
constantly comparing yourself with whomever you
deem as the best, studying their hits, analyzing their
misses.

> It's funny, before I even made music, I was the
> biggest Timbaland fan, [a] huge Timbaland fan. [I]
> didn't make music, wasn't thinking about it, and
> I used to listen to all the sounds he used and all
> the innovative things he was doing, and I was just
> [like], "I love it!" So when I started making music,
> it was like, he's the one that impressed me the most.

> *I need to be as good [as], if not better than, him.* So,
> I would remake something he did or I would just
> constantly use him as the bar, [to the] point where
> I started making stuff that I thought was as good
> and sometimes better. It was just a goal; it wasn't
> even that I want[ed] to be great so I could be rich,
> or I want[ed] to be great because of any other
> reason than just for myself, and I think [that was]
> just me being competitive. In anything I've ever
> done—producing, drawing, or designing—it's just
> like, "*I want to be the best. As good as I [can] possibly
> be.*" —REO of the Soundkillers

By benchmarking yourself against your greats,
you can inspire a fiery competition with your idols
that pushes the boundaries of your creativity. REO's
mark, the legendary Timbaland, provided him with
the kind of target that meant he would need to become extraordinary just to get close.

Fresh Sounds

> What are the sounds that might stand out? What's
> the new software out? What's new, what's updated,
> what's next, what's the latest? —Dow, Tha Bizness

Dow stressed that keeping up on the cutting edge
of production technology and new sounds is critical
to Tha Bizness's production success. I was terrible at
keeping pace with technology and the latest sounds.
For much of my brief career, my drums and sounds
were half dead on a stretcher, and until somebody
embarrassed me and pointed them out lying life-

less in my music, I rarely hunted for the latest and greatest sounds. When I was on Logic and Reason, my sound selection sucked, and it was reflected in my beats. Conference after conference, beat battle after beat battle, track dump after track dump, individual instrument sound is a consistent serial killer lying in the shadows waiting to grab and slaughter producers.

> Get out of the stuff that's in the keyboard; learn how to tweak your sounds. I always have to bring this up. Khalil is one of my favorite producers, he works in Reason, but if you listen to his stuff, it's so big and it's so powerful and he *tweaks every sound; he knows how to make them sound dated; he knows how to make them sound futuristic, whatever.* Learn how to tweak your stuff; learn how to try different sounds, different textures. Try different things and be original. —Focus

I warned you earlier about the comfort in doing the minimum. To ascend to that next level, to add that flavor of uniqueness, to essentially think outside the boombox, you have to attack your tracks at the level of individual sounds. But you begin by taking the time to tweak the things that others won't even bother to manipulate. Rich sounds are a powerful piece of production, and mastery over sound selection can really set you apart. When I was selecting beats to shop to labels, the one thing that would stop me in my tracks and make me pay attention was the

inclusion of a unique, crispy sound. It's a very com-
manding part of your music.

Work Ethic

> It's just like working out, like going to the gym
> every day; you're not gonna get the body that you
> want or the strength that you want just by chilling.
> You just gotta work out. —Dow, Tha Bizness

Like going to the gym every day. Every. Day. Constant. Relentless. Determined. Dogged. Daily work.
No days off, Ferris Bueller!

> Doing something creative every day—that's your
> job. [That] doesn't even mean making a beat. [It can
> be] learning a chord progression, digging through
> records, finding another piece of gear, going to
> someone else's studio and listening. Constantly
> learning every day. That's your job. Be creative and
> learn more about your craft every day. —DJ Khalil

I love that Khalil included going to someone else's
studio and listening. We're going to talk about how
powerful that is later on.

> [Employ] daily training regimens just to better
> yourself. Every time you turn around and make
> a beat, you *listen to it* because, if you're a real
> producer, you're not just gonna make a beat and
> just move on to the next thing. You're [going
> to] listen to it, see how you can better it, maybe
> learn how to tweak the mix so that that beat is
> conveyed to everyone the exact way you hear it in
> [your] head. That's how you better yourself daily.

> That's how you turn around and make sure that you *become*. You perfect your craft, and you *become* a great producer. —Focus

I'm always wary of beatmakers who run off at the mouth about knocking out some ridiculous number of tracks a day: "Fifteen tracks finished today! I'm doing it, baby!" And it's only 2:17 p.m. I mean, I'm all for being prolific; as I said earlier, it's an important piece of sustaining a career. However, how can you devote tender, loving care to your music with such an assembly-line state of mind? I think what Focus says is critical in the evolution from beatmaker to producer; the ability to sit back and analyze your music before hastily moving on to the next thing is vital.

> Some people may work all day to come out of the tank and equal this amount of greatness. Some people may not work as hard and still get that same amount out of the tank, plus more. So, it's still based on talent. This is a talent-based industry. You gotta have the talent. Everybody just thinks that just because I can get the money, I can go buy the equipment—that still doesn't give you the talent that's behind some of these guys. Some of these producers are really talented. —Chuck Greene, 1 Shot Management

I'm glad that Chuck brought up this point. Because it's so easy to just go get equipment, and it's such a popular thing to do nowadays, we overlook talent. If you have a special knack for music, that God-given gift, then yes, the road can look different. Now, this isn't to say that if you don't have the natural gift that you can't find success. You just need to outwork the people who do have the natural talent. *Your work ethic needs to be your natural talent:*

> Hard work pays off for you. That's just straight up. Like, really try to become a master. It may take you a little longer than the next guy, but one thing, he's not gonna outwork you—*you* have a work ethic like no other. We party, or we bullshit on top of our work, hang out, [pursue] women, [or] play games, versus that one guy who says "f*ck that, I'm about to engulf this." This is the drive; this is the passion. Keep working, and it will pay off. —Chuck Greene, 1 Shot Management

Self-explanatory advice from the manager of one of the hottest and most revolutionary production groups of the last decade.

> You have to have an open mind, [be] willing to listen, learn, and work hard. I'm my own worst critic, so I'm always striving. I'm not even close to where I want to be. *And I have to get to that point.* —DJ Khalil

This is an idea that Tha Bizness also touched on, the notion of continuously working and striving toward greatness, even at this point in their careers. Do you know what kind of incredible focus and determination you have to possess in order to tell me you're

"not even close" to where you want to be creatively
when you've *already* worked with some of the biggest
artists on earth, including Aloe Blacc, Jay-Z, and
Eminem, and you're still eager to put in the work
to get better? You're competing against people who
have *that level of desire for greatness* when you're out
there building your career. You can't lose being that
hungry. That's insane. DJ Khalil is a beast.

Think Outside the (Boom)Box

> [It's] funny how people go crazy over something
> that's different. [There's] a bunch of sheep out
> here. Be creative and try to stand out. Even if it's
> one sound. —Needlz

In addition to the need for continuous improvement, Needlz stresses the importance of being unique.
We're the ones sitting at a judge's table during these
beat battles and receiving countless beats to critique,
astonished by how much producers sound like clones
of each other. It can be difficult to step out of the
box. I've been there myself—I know what it feels like
to leave that unusual beat off the beat CD because
you're scared. You know that you have to treat every
opportunity as special, and you don't want to fail by
coming out of left field with something too unique.
You also know the industry gets a bad case of tunnel
vision, with many tastemakers demanding a replica
of the popular sound of the moment: "Man, that's

great. But, uh, gimme a track that sounds exactly like such-and-such." With requests like that, it's easy to get caught up in being a soft, cuddly sheep, blindly following the flock. But we know of the rewards that can come when you bring your own unique flavor.

Balance

> Be flexible in trying to find ways to make "them" happy. Gotta make sure the customer is satisfied. —Needlz

Excellence is also about remembering that this is commerce, and you're providing a service to the market. You're building a product to fit the customer's needs. You've got to keep the artists, managers, and labels happy, and sometimes that means removing yourself from the equation and making sure everyone else gets what they need. Sometimes.

> Sometimes you just gotta say f*ck it, and make what feels good to you. There are a lot of times we'll go through maybe two weeks, three weeks of making beats, and they may not even be for what we're working on right now, but they'll just feel good, and we'll find a home for them later. A lot of cats just get burned out because they just keep trying to satisfy everybody else, and it's like, at some point, you try to satisfy yourself, and it'll become a lot more fun and a lot easier to do. And as long as the beats are cool, shit, you'll be straight. —Dow, Tha Bizness

On the other hand, maintain the love and joy of production by leaving room to work on what you want to work on. It can quickly become very drab and job-like if you're constantly satisfying other parties and you forget about you. Balance is crucial. Wonderful advice for those of you who get through the door and want to stay mentally healthy while you're in the building.

> One thing I had to learn was, when everybody's like, "Yo, we want you to do this kind of pop music," and you want to be like, "No, that's not what I want to do, I'm creative, I want to do [this]," and they're just like, "If you do what we want and it's successful, then you can [use] all of your time doing whatever you want." But I was such a purist: "No, I'm not gonna do that, I'm not gonna sell out...." But I think that over the years I learned that it's not necessarily selling out. It's a business, and you're doing what you gotta do to continue getting money in order to make what you want to make or put out the artists that you want to. You have to consider [that] two or three days out of your week [are like] going to a desk job: "I'm going here, I'm gonna make *this* music, [then] I'm gonna clock out." And the next three days, you go in and you just say, "Hey, I'm gonna make whatever I wanna make." Creating that balance, I think that's something I had to add. —REO of the Soundkillers

Much of this is about growth; it's about evolution. Do you see how REO evolved as a businessman and learned an effective way to balance his creative output so he could further his career?

Collaboration

DJ Khalil offers some of the most powerful information I've ever heard regarding collaboration as it pertains to us producers. We were discussing the lone-wolf nature of production today. Khalil's vision of production is opposite the norm:

> The way you make music is not one person sitting in a room with a computer or a machine.... Music is made with multiple [people] in the room bringing perspective. That's production. Quincy Jones knew to get this drummer, and Rod Temperton, he knew exactly which songwriters, which musicians, whatever creative people he needed. He may not be writing the song, but he knew how to put it together. That's what a producer does, traditionally. [It] feels like that's the way it's supposed to be. [It] shouldn't be solo. —DJ Khalil

Here's a concept that's key to DJ Khalil's creativity and success. He believes wholeheartedly in collaboration, and I love and share his philosophy. The production community has a serious problem with this concept of one person sitting in a studio creating everything behind the beat. It's funny that things have evolved this way, because as we know from the records we sample, music was never made like this. When you flip over the LP sleeve, there's an army of arrangers, composers, producers, programmers, and musicians—people who each contributed their own musical genius toward creating those magical four-bar moments you had to cut a piece from. Not only this, but our biggest producers of the past and present are collaborators. Your favorites work with a team, each team member bringing his or her expertise and experience to the production table to co-create a musical moment in time.

I, too, was caught up in the lone-wolf syndrome—me, myself, and I, stuck in a room—and I suffered for it. I stupidly thought I was devaluing myself by "needing" someone else to come in and work on a beat with me. I wish I could have seen how my ego held me back. If only I'd known then what I know now.

DJ Khalil also discussed the importance of working with people of similar mindsets, hunger, and focus, intent on evolving and comfortable with collaboration. Don't collaborate just for the sake of collaboration. As you seek people to create with, know that chemistry is important; you must invite the right kind of person into your creative world. And be sure to properly mind the business of collaboration. That means laying out beforehand the terms of the collaboration: filling out split sheets, knowing who owns masters and publishing, etc. Address the business side and have terms on paper so that a great creative relationship doesn't get mauled by the fangs of business.

THE FINAL MIX

This law about striving for production excellence evolved significantly over the years it took to write this book. It began as a law that was more theoretical, but it turned into what it is now, which is essentially a guidepost with wisdom from some of the best. This is one of my favorite laws because you can spend years using these techniques: emulating other artists, studying the legends and greats, re-creating records, practicing multiple genres and styles, analyzing released records, benchmarking against the competition, learning how to select the right sounds, and learning to collaborate. Use everything you've read in this chapter to help you practice your skills daily and master your craft.

One last thought before we conclude. I learned a concept from self-help guru Zig Ziglar that will help you as you make your way through this business. When I was in my motivational-audio-CD stage, Zig was explaining the notion that in a restaurant, you get your meal and then you pay. But in the hunt for success, life is like a cafeteria, where you pay for your food first and then you eat.

This was a concept I'd forgotten and become disconnected from until Felisha Booker reminded me years later. Production is a "pay first" reality. My question to you is this: how long can you pay the price without being able to eat the meal? Can you use the techniques in this chapter to work on your craft, practice excellence, drill day in and day out for three, five, seven, or even ten years without becoming discouraged? How long can you go without reaping the benefits of your work?

Like many things I've discussed, "pay first" is an overlooked concept when it comes to making music, but it's an undeniable truth. Many of the producers we look up to are in the positions they're in because they were able to do the things you've read about in this chapter—hold on as long as possible, remain patient, and stay cool as a snowstorm, all while mastering their craft. I violated this principle. I was constantly frustrated, and if I'd been as smart then as I am now, I would have shut my mouth and continued to work. I now know that you must absolutely persist! So, how long are you willing to stand in line, and how much are you willing to pay before you can eat your meal?

When you give to your craft, it always comes back.
—DJ Khalil

LAW 17

Work the Network: Put the Same Effort into Networking and Hustling Beats As You Do into Making Them

OBSERVATION

I don't care what you do or who you are—the ancient art known as networking cannot be escaped. Your network is the lubrication that greases the gears of the machine that is success. As a producer, you must be able to build a strong network to succeed.

Me? Oh, I was pure idiot when it came to networking. Back when I was shooting music videos and aspiring to produce, I was horrible at introducing myself to people to let them know what I did. My mouth wired itself shut when it should have been open. I was terrified of simply walking up to people and saying, "What's good? What's your name? What are you doing here?"

I'd be standing next to artists who needed tracks, and it wouldn't even dawn on me to meet and pow-wow so I could get them some music. If it did dawn on me, I would sit there and mull it over, rolling out a full mental construction crew to build me a bit of courage before finally assuring myself that I was capable of speaking to such-and-such person. Sometimes, I'd procrastinate so damn long that the person I intended to introduce myself to got up and bounced. After so much of this, I began to drink my own pessimistic-flavored Kool-Aid and convinced myself that I would always be shy, an introvert, and a poor networker. And that was just who I was going to be.

REALIZATION

Let me tell you how destructive a decision like that can be for you. If you're a dreamer, one of the worst things you can do to yourself is willingly guzzle down your own negative Kool-Aid. *Once you've decided that you "are" something, then that's what you'll be. Your behavior and actions will sync up with your belief about yourself, and you will become what you prophesied.*

Phase 1: Fear

Poor networking typically arises from some sort of fear—fear of rejection or fear of success, perhaps the fear of disappointment. Point being, there is something identifiable—and fixable—in your head that prevents you from meeting people. Look deep inside and analyze what's *behind* the reason for your poor networking. What are you afraid of? Whatever that fear may be, investigate it, become acquainted with it, then walk brazenly toward it and sock it in the face. Slowly begin working on yourself: develop confidence in the fact that *you are capable* of meeting anyone in a room. Start the process by introducing yourself to one or two people at an event. Eventually, you'll see that it's not the nightmare you've made it out to be. And you'll begin to conquer the underlying fear behind your poor networking. This is how we evolve, by charging bravely in the direction of what scares the hell out of us.

You are capable, and you must be a competent networker and relationship-builder to get off the ground. I don't want to sound like one of those overly enthusiastic networking gurus who make it sound like you can conquer your fear of networking in a quick series of easy steps, because it is a challenge. Just do me a favor and start. Everyone can start small.

As far as my own abysmal networking, there was an underlying fear lurking in the shadows—I wasn't confident in my work. A fear of being called a no-talent hack was living like a filthy squatter in the back of my unguarded mind. I wasn't confident in my catalog or my ability to *consistently* deliver heat. So I was quiet and shy. I hate that I made a subconscious decision like that; I could have gotten a few beats off and purged a lot of self-doubt, thus refueling my spirit with confidence and a newfound desire to succeed. But I wrecked myself.

Think about it. When you're dope, what can anybody tell you? Being an amazing producer makes you want to whip out a megaphone and shout from the rooftops. You want everybody to know how immensely talented you are. But when you set your standards too high or don't give yourself adequate time to improve, you're never good enough in your own eyes. The end result is that you become a mute, standing by the wall at some industry event like a cheap coat rack, jealously watching everyone else make connections. Then, when you leave the event, the bell rings and you commence a boxing match by throwing swift jabs of guilt at yourself because you feel like you've let yourself down.

This is why it's imperative to master the craft: your skill level becomes one less thing to get hung up on when it comes time to network.

Phase 2: Maintenance, Man

After you've conquered your fears and become comfortable with shaking hands and kissing babies, the next level of networking is the development and maintenance of your relationships. Meeting people eventually becomes easy—leaving an event with a million handshakes and a stack of business cards becomes normal. Building and maintaining relationships with your contacts to the point where you have rapport is the next step. And then getting someone to stop what they're doing in the middle of their busy day and help *you* is a whole different ballgame.

This is when your business practices, personality, and patience need to be on point. People avoid working with assholes and egomaniacs (although they somehow always seem to find their way to the top, or do they play the game and then revert to being assholes once they've reached a certain position?). People work with other people they like—business is personal. Represent yourself in the best light; look for ways to help those you're networking with. Be genuine. Ask your contacts what you can do for them; help them with something they need, and the good-networking karma will return to you. Check up on people every so often. See how people are doing. Take interest in their interests. If they have kids, ask how they are. Be as interesting as possible. The more things you're into or passionate about, the easier it is to relate to different types of people. Even though I've had to work on my relationship building, I have a diverse set of interests, so I'm capable of sustaining conversations with any- and everyone: music industry folks, cats from the 'hood, old white guys I meet at the airport, little old ladies, and everyone in between. I find common ground, and I stay on it.

Don't make beats like me. You cannot afford to go another day without building relationships with people and finding ways to help them get where they're trying to go, people who in turn will help you get to your destination. It starts with a sincere belief in the power of networking, knowing that you are capable and knowing that there's always room to improve. If success is what you seek, you don't have a choice.

Networking to Move Music

It dawned on me during an editing session of this book that I needed to elaborate a bit further on this networking discussion. Producers network for a specific purpose, and I have to frame the discussion to fit that purpose. You aren't out there meeting people and introducing yourself to find players for poker night or a wingman to hit the bar with. You need to sell tracks. Hustling music is a tough subject to tackle, and I was far from the best, so I won't rely only on myself to tell you how to do it. On the other end of the spectrum, most of the producers I've spoken with are so far in the game, their brands sell beats for them. Tha Bizness was a bit of an exception to that, being only a few years deep into the heavy-name-recognition phase when I interviewed them. The hustle was still vivid and fresh, and they had a lot of wisdom to offer.

I offer you a list of must-do actions from a variety of sources with exceptional beat-hustling skills. These pieces of wisdom are from producers I know who put as much work into moving beats as they do into making them. Because, as Dow says, "The same hustle you have in making your beats, you gotta have the same hustle in getting them off."

Hen began by saying, "Learning to interact with the artist and learning to provide him with a service, that's what made us cool." It takes time to speak an artist's language, to learn how to work with them and provide a service while building a relationship. It's an art in itself and hard to do. Use every chance you get to sharpen your ability to provide great service while creating a bond with your collaborators.

Dow reflects,

A lot of producers, one, they don't have a personality; two, they don't get up and leave [the studio]. ...Producers are just comfortable; they're comfortable in the studio just making stuff. And it's like, they don't know how to go out and just meet anybody. You just really gotta click and appeal [to artists]. We've always had that *likeability*, and it's never really been a problem.

Producers enjoy basking in the studio. It's a haven, a warm, cozy bubble with soft kitten fur for walls. Going out to meet people means you have to leave your haven, where things are easy and it's just you and the music. As Dow says, you have to be able to venture into the cold. And you must develop and be able to use your likeability to connect with people. At the base of any business is the human connection. Being cool and likeable is extremely valuable as a producer, who is essentially a salesman, trying to move products.

Says Dow,

> From my DJ side, it's keeping an eye on what's going on and who are the new guys, and luckily our guesses on who's gonna pop have been pretty much on, from Drake to even, like, the new young dudes out here.... Just by having that vision and messing with them early.... Even like Wiz Khalifa, we did a song with Wiz Khalifa like in '08 when he was still on Warner Bros. and they didn't know what do to with him. But we knew at the time, man, he's dope.

You can never underestimate the role that vision plays in a producer's career. You can completely blow open the door to success by gluing yourself to the right artist's rocket boosters while being sonically prepared for what comes next. Time and time again, we've seen producers enjoy a meteoric rise by producing an unknown artist who suddenly becomes known. Do your best to identify, network with, and work with those dope cats you have a gut feeling about. You just never know.

Dow explained, "And you gotta have that relationship with that artist so that he feels comfortable f*cking with you, and then it can be just his good chemistry and it goes." Many artists are already strange to begin with; maybe it was part of the deal while bartering with God for an extra helping of creativity. On top of being odd, they've been hunted by grabby friends, family, and industry vampires, many seeking to wring them dry of riches like frayed washrags. As people who can be on the defense about whom they trust, they react like puppies who have been whacked repeatedly with rolled-up newspapers. Flinching when you come around despite your good intentions, they need time to learn they can trust you. Getting in good with artists to make them feel comfortable working with you is a skill you should seek to master.

Dow continued with,

> That's what it's all about; if you give that artist that feeling, like, man, this is gonna be the one, shit, they'll get behind it and just do it. It'll be their favorite song because they were sold on the dream, and they really liked it.

Once you develop that skill, and the puppy now comes to lick your hand instead of flinching, you must not forget that you're not just a producer: you're a salesman, too. And enthusiasm moves product. So often, beats move because of the producer's ability to make people believe in the power of his tracks. Enthusiasm and belief are contagious in a room full of people. Don't go to sessions or meetings without them.

Hen says,

> Dow will stay in the studio from eight to eight just shooting the shit with cats when I'll be like, "Man,

I can't do it." But he might have a little bit more patience than me, just to build the relationships with cats, just so that our placements and some of the things we need done, get done.

Sometimes, moving beats or any other product or service just takes a little "shooting the shit." For those of you unfamiliar with the term, it describes sitting around conversing about random things, chilling, and building a relationship in the process. While this can be an incredible investment of time, you benefit when your clients walk away from one of these instances thinking, "Man, that MayDay is a cool-ass dude. I'm gonna have to listen to those beats he gave me."

Advises Ric Spicer of Sweatbeatz Productions,

Be patient. I've been in this beat-dealing game for years now, and we are just seeing some of the fruit from the seeds we planted when we started. Be patient. Dead serious. Kanye West, Polow da Don, will.i.am—all were in the background grinding for years before they were "put on." It's called paying dues. Very few skip this step.

Practicing patience as a hustler of music means taming a two-headed beast. We discussed the internal part, creative patience, in the chapter on excellence. You must be patient with the external side, too: matters outside of yourself that you can't control, such as circumstances and people. Things rarely move quite as fast as we'd like in the music business, and you have to be patient when dealing with people and trying to sell music. I used to get very pissed with people who didn't move as quickly as I liked, and I took it as an insult when things weren't accomplished in a time frame I thought reasonable. Instead of keeping cool and dismissing things that were out of my control, here I was, willingly giving up my peace and power to someone else.

Also, I had an asshole mentality and refused to invest time in building relationships with people so we could eventually do business. I was devoid of patience, and I felt emasculated having to chase around grown men to build recognition and grow a relationship. It was frustrating and seemed like a waste of energy to have to spend hours in someone's presence in the hopes of getting some future work. And then repeat the process for several weeks afterward, constantly popping in, keeping the face fresh, being around until the guy who calls the shots says, "Who's that? What does he do? Bring him in."

But for some people and opportunities, that's exactly what it takes. My former business partner, Will, is the king of remaining patient to get some eventual business done. He realizes that movers and shakers have dozens of hungry souls drooling at the thought of soliciting business from them. Many decision-makers simply aren't willing to break bread with cats they don't know. By having patience with this process, you can open huge doors after a level of comfort and trust develops in a professional relationship—what I failed to realize when I was hustling beats. I didn't have the patience to just chill with an artist, day after day, before I whipped out my beat CD. I didn't have the wisdom to deal with people *as people*, understand who they were *first*, so I could bless them with some music *second*.

Once you are successful at building the relationship and it is time to play music, play damn good music. There's nothing worse than going through all that work to finally get in the door, finally get the opportunity to get in the studio, and not have both a high-quality product and a high-quality product that *fits the customer's needs*. If you don't know where your skill level is—you assume you're a lot hotter than you actually are—that's how you ruin opportunities.

Take it from Fuego, equally talented as a producer and salesman: "Don't push tracks unless they are undeniable. There is nothing worse than getting an A&R's attention and then playing him some wack shit. If you do that, you're done in his eyes." I call Fuego my white, German brother because we have strangely similar tastes in rare, funky music and dystopian sci-fi films. Fuego's one of the most talented beat-hustlers I've ever known. Many times I've stood in awe of this cat, watching him fly from Germany to

the U.S. several times a year and build bridges with
the precision of a veteran contractor. It's even more
impressive to watch this European cat come through
with his thick German accent and completely eclipse
the hustle of people who live in the U.S. 365 days a
year. And he follows his own advice—his product is
always bananas. It was essential that I get some of
his thoughts to pass along to you.

Ric says,

> Rappers, singers, and A&Rs want beats with hooks
> and full songs more than ever. Even if the hook
> isn't chosen, it gives the listener an idea of the
> appropriate artists or outlets to get the music to.
> These cats are a little lazy now, so make it as easy
> as possible for them to pick your music.

I think this became the trend in the mid-2000s. I
of limited vision never looked up from my MPC and
noticed that collaborating with writers to develop
more appealing tracks and songs was essential to
playing by the new rules. As Dow told me, people
don't have five-star-restaurant patience today: "It's a
drive-through business, so you gotta have your little
meals ready, or shit, you're gonna be out of business."
Much of industry (consumers, too) has neither the
time nor the palette for a five-course meal. Instead
of artists or A&Rs figuring it all out by themselves,
you'll have to bring more of a finished product to the
table today. And hooks and full songs are essential to

the pre-prep, drive-through mentality. Keep in mind, with this being the current standard, you've got to be just as good at producing hooks and full songs as you are at creating instrumentals. It sucks to receive a dope track with an awful hook or song or a bad mix on the vocals. *Present-day circumstances require that you be better skilled at more pieces of the production puzzle.*

THE FINAL MIX

I remember feeling a certain way about the music industry, which contributed to my horrible networking. I didn't want to play the game with people who weren't like me. I tried to avoid snakes, backstabbers, false prophets, paper gangsters, and the profoundly ignorant like they were Ebola. I'm an extremely genuine dude. None of that foolishness is my style.

Some of you may feel the same way. The entertainment business is bursting at the seams with the morally bankrupt, with swine that enjoy getting filthy, and you will encounter and deal with them in your pursuit of production happiness. You're going to have to carefully hopscotch through the industry to avoid being maimed by a landmine of a person. If you want to be an extraordinary producer, you won't have a choice but to deal with unsavory people. But don't be like me and just write off the whole process because of the snakes, assholes, and gangsters in the business.

Not all of your connections will be amazing, but you'll meet some incredible people along the journey. Good people swim together in the music industry like schools of fish. They are life-giving pockets of air that save us from drowning in business. And some of these people will be friends for life—a good thought to focus on while you're out there swimming, avoiding great white sharks.

Also remember, it's not just about networking; it's also about whom you're networking with. Not everyone is worth your precious time and energy. There are certain cliques in this business that, should you be lucky enough to network your way into them, will propel you light years ahead of the average Joe.

Chuck Greene says,

> You can find out who's live and who's not by asking others. Because of their past, ... if you're in those live cities, you'll know by asking if that person is a player or not. If you're not [in] a shaking city, it's a little harder; you gotta have a gut feeling.

Ask yourself: Who is this person I'm dealing with, and whom is he connected to? It's like playing skee ball; not everybody is a one-hundred-point toss. Try to weed out some of the clowns spouting empty promises and look for the money ball.

Chuck offered more wisdom about networking within the industry. When you're seeking out and networking with people who are in a so-called position to move beats, Chuck warns against "signing [your] shit away to these people." He wants you cats to know that people who move beats from one place to another are bridge-builders and nothing more. They should be paid by their ability to move an item from place to place. Chuck continued with, "If I tell you it costs to ride to [the] bridge, the bridge shouldn't own your property. That's not a good guy already. That's one of the biggest things I see; ... instead of a person who has a bridge taking a percentage, they want ownership." And ownership is everything in this game. It's what gives the lions of the jungle their roar. People like these are game hunters in the industry jungle; they patiently lie camouflaged behind a bush and wait for unsuspecting producers. After you've reached for the opportunity and sprung the trap, you're cooked into a tasty meal, and your head is mounted on a wall with your face frozen into a puzzled expression that says, "What in the hell happened here?" Critical to your success is the development of a sixth sense about people and circumstances. As you grow wiser and educate yourself on business principles, you'll learn to spot human landmines like a single, rotting tooth in an otherwise healthy smile.

This law resonates with me so much because poor networking is a costly mistake that so many of us make daily. I've been to many events and conferences, and I'd ask the producers who paid several hundred dollars to attend, fly out, get a room, and feed themselves during their trip, "Who did you meet today?" Too often their eyes fell to their shoelaces like a child in trouble, and they'd bashfully murmur, "Nobody." I'd shake my head in disbelief, saying, "All of these panelists, A&Rs, producers, publishers, music supervisors, PRO execs, and you met no one? Why are you here?" ("PROs" are performance rights organizations. You're gonna need to know that.) Nothing can cripple you like subpar networking. I've been there, watching my opportunities disintegrate as a result.

Disclaimer

Though your network is extremely important, some of you may need to employ other techniques to build it. Not all of you are natural social butterflies. Not all of you are witty masters of small talk. Not all of you have a stockpile of clever jokes or interesting stories, or are baby-bottom smooth during conversation. Unfortunately, some of you are weird, awkward, and ignorant, and would probably do better by keeping your mouth shut. It's all right, not a problem. If you are completely inept and awkward, then you have one more possible option. You need to bust your ass to find someone to speak on your behalf. Find that person who's the social butterfly of the crew, and let him do the smooth talking for you while you keep quiet and focus on making magic in the studio. You'd be surprised at how many successful producers employ this technique, either because they choose to or because they must. But there are only two roads here: learn to network or pay someone else!

LAW 18

A Business, Man: Add Business to Your Recipe for Success

Understand that this is a business *at the beginning of the day*, not at the end of the day. —Chuck Greene, 1 Shot Management

As I spill my guts about my many mistakes, you all must be thinking that I was crazy. *"This guy here sure did a lot of silly stuff."* I sure did. This is what it looks like when you boil down twenty-something years of habit, mediocre thinking, and music production into one book. But now you will avoid these mistakes. In retrospect, I believe that my destiny was to fall madly in love with production, make the worst decisions possible, and snap rules like twigs only to create a sturdy foundation for this book. If I'd executed many of these things perfectly, there would be no basis for me to pass along what I've learned. I'd be busy producing and wouldn't have the time or perspective needed to write this book. So, in the end, we both win. Let's continue in the spirit of avoiding my mistakes with a look at the business side of things.

OBSERVATION

Back when I was in the midst of being a beatmaker, I was only about the creative process—the art, the composition, the sounds, and the melodies. I couldn't tell you a damn thing about what was supposed to happen when it came time to do business. I was lost in a dark, dank cave of my own business ignorance. How does publishing work? Hell, for that matter, what was publishing? Uh, a split sheet? Licensing? What are the basics of the producer agreement? How much should I charge for a beat? What kind of producer royalties am I owed, and who's responsible for paying them? How are they calculated? At what point do I send over the files? Who's responsible for clearing the sample, and who's legally liable if that person doesn't?

I had no team, no business mentors, no attorney, I wasn't signed to a performance rights organization (PRO)—I had nothing. As a matter of fact, back then, I didn't even know what a PRO was. Was a PRO a publisher? It took me a few years to figure out that the American PROs—SESAC, BMI, and ASCAP—aren't publishers, although they distribute publishing. If somebody had walked up to me and said, "MayDay, we'd like to purchase this track. We'll send the paperwork over, and we'd like you to track out the session files," I would have been ecstatic at

first and then nervous because I wouldn't have had a
clue what I was supposed to do next. *And I probably
would have gotten jerked.* Even though I wasn't anywhere near the creative level that I desired, I was still
good enough to sell a beat at any moment. I would
have been completely unprepared and in a prime position to be hustled.

REALIZATION

I hope that in this age when information flows freely
like the wind, you're smarter than I was and you've
sharpened your production-business knowledge. But
it amazes me how much producers don't learn, think
they don't have to learn, and blatantly ignore. This *is*
business. You need to have a great understanding of
everything pertaining to your ability to earn income
in this business. Why? The less you know, the more
money you leave on the table. Yes, sitting there, a
nice stack of cash, looking at you like you're a dumb-
ass, because it could have been sitting comfortably
in your checking account. But no, you didn't know
that you could have argued a better deal. You didn't
do your research and don't know you shortchanged
yourself on your up-front fees.

As Hen explains,

> It's like a recipe, right? [If] you want to bake a cake,
> you need this, you need this, you need this, ... you
> need a quarter cup of this, a teaspoon of this, or

whatever. We look at everything as a recipe.... When we said, "Okay, we want to be great producers, what does it take?" You gotta know the business. So, what does that mean? You gotta know what a producer does. You gotta know how a producer gets paid, how many different types of deals you can make. Even when we really didn't understand it, like, "What do you mean publishing, you can look at it as 200 percent? What does that even mean?" We had to *keep looking at it, keep reading it, keep looking at it over and over again, until it just became like a language*.... Like, yeah, we understand those deals, we understand how we get paid, we understand the types of deals that are out there for us. *So we studied that, just like we studied everything else.* It's really just about studying.

Pick up a book. Go to a conference (as many Dynamic Producer members faithfully did while I worked there). Understand how you get paid, who's responsible for paying you. What deal points should you be looking for? What should you consider when you're searching for an attorney? What interests should your attorney have in mind for you? How are points calculated? What is a point? How does the PRO know to be looking out for your music? What is music licensing? Should you sign a publishing deal? If so, under what circumstances? How many song commitments should you agree to for what amount of money? What about a production deal with a record label? What happens when you collaborate with multiple producers and songwriters? How do you avoid getting jerked? What if you've done work on an album and it gets shelved and you got only half of your fee? Can a good manager take care of many of these issues for you? Sure. What about an attorney? Absolutely. But do you want to try to build a career while remaining ignorant of how your money is calculated? Hen explains,

> So for us, handling the business, we knew that if we had to rely completely on a manager or completely on a lawyer to tell us exactly what we need to do business-wise, we [could] always get taken advantage of.... So we had to learn everything about the whole game, as much as we could, from the books or whatever.

Find me one successful CEO who doesn't know what his CFO, legal team, and COO are doing at all times. Intelligent business owners have an intimate knowledge of the inner workings of their companies and how money is earned. They're educated enough to study their companies and look for important information about the health of the business at any moment, or have conversations with the people who manage certain aspects of the business.

I know that you have to focus on your creativity and churn out records, but you must have enough knowledge to either examine what's going on with your business or have an intelligent conversation with your team. *That's your livelihood and your future.* There's no company-sponsored 401K or health insurance for music producers, and we damn sure don't get company stock. If you make music for a living, your ability to master the details of the business, which influences your ability to master the kinds of deals at your disposal, will account for a significant portion of your revenue. You better damn well know the business behind every dollar and cent if you're going to do this for the long haul and eat from the fruit of your labor when you're fifty years old.

Hen explains how Tha Bizness works their business:

> For a new cat, you just go on the Internet and figure out anything, and they might have a YouTube video explaining it to you even easier. The game is completely changed from when we first got into it, ... but it still remains the same; you have to understand what it is that you're getting into and learn everything about it. ... We just learned it all, as much as we could, and continued to learn it over and over again until it became second nature, and [we] handle our business accordingly.

> That's why when we did the song deals for certain cats, we approached them with the deal—"You like all these beats, let's do a song deal." *We didn't wait for them to ask us to do it; we already knew that was a situation we could get done* without being superinvolved in their camp like a production deal. The difference between a production deal and song deal—... you gotta know the differences....

> You should know that if [you're] getting started, and [you] want to get down with a label or team and they offer [you] a production deal, that's usually

gonna entail them taking 50 percent of everything
you do. But they're gonna push you into their camp
and brand you as one of *their* ... producers and put
you on *their* artists. So they're gonna take 50 percent
of your publishing, 50 percent of your advance, and
in most cases, 50 percent of everything that you do.

In a song deal, it's like, okay, you like these beats,
[but] I don't have to be necessarily tied to your
camp. Not that ... we didn't want to be with any
certain team or whatever, but our thing was ... we
want to make music for everybody, we want to work
with everybody, we just want to have fun and get
... heard all over the place. So that was kind of the
best approach, being able to do a deal that shows
them some love. They feel like ... "These guys are
working with us," but at the same time, it still kind
of gives us our freedom so we can go and still try to
achieve all the goals that we had set for ourselves
many moons ago.

I've heard of horror stories from producers who
just didn't know and, as a result, could have been
eating off a lot of money that was just left behind.
You think shady people are going to tell you that
you're about to miss out on sweet, juicy revenue?
That snake won't think twice about handing you a
work-for-hire agreement if you don't know what it is
and there's a chance you'll sign it. People are looking
out for their own interests in all walks of life, but
especially in *this* business. It is your responsibility, no
one else's, to learn and understand. "The music industry is an animal that eats its young," CeeLo Green

has said.[1] *You are a business, man.* Join a production community, hit a seminar, research online. Take a well-known manager or lawyer to lunch to pick his brain, or pay him his hourly rate to have him break down essentials, the cost of which would be far less than mistakes made in ignorance.

REO can vouch for the importance of educating yourself on the business end:

> You know, honestly, attending some of those Dynamic Producer things put me onto a lot—having a lawyer come and talk about the legal aspect of music, having other professionals come in and share their experiences and explain to you what things were—all really helped educate me when I didn't know what to do.

> My manager's also my business partner, so I handle a lot of the creative music, and he handles a lot of the business side. We're mainly self-taught and really kind of learned the ropes together but have had some amazing mentors along the way. It's great to have people you trust in your corner to understand you and help fight for what is yours.

> There's this famous quote that says, "You don't get what you deserve, you get what you negotiate." That's so true in this business—there are no rules. *There's no fair, there's no unfair, it's what you fight for.* It's just really important that you

---

1   Lauria, Peter, "Cee Lo Uncensored." *The Daily Beast. News-week,* 19 January 2011. Web: 20 January 2011. <http://www.the-dailybeast.com/articles/2011/01/19/cee-lo-uncensored-on-grammys-dixie-chicks-billy-joel-and-maroon-5.html>

acknowledge some sort of wiser counsel before you make any decision. And just try to stay as knowledgeable as you can because [that's] what's gonna get you paid.

There's too much information floating around today for you to be clueless. Maximize some of the tools that REO just laid out for you. Unless you've got a good manager and an attorney you absolutely trust with your life, sit down and learn for yourself. Even if you've got that type of manager or attorney, still learn.

Once you begin to comprehend how the business works and the money flows, you can create a better vision of what kind of business and income opportunities are available (as Tha Bizness just demonstrated by preemptively approaching artists with song deals instead of signing production deals).

The smart producers who've done their homework know where to focus and can build business models and generate substantial income streams because they understand the puzzle pieces they're working with and the ways they fit together. Do you want to eat off of production forever? You can create revenue that will continue to flow long after you're in a box, benefiting the generations of family after you. These are the amazing possibilities of long-term wealth in the music business. Learn these puzzle pieces of information so you can see the big picture. Become a business, man.

Survive the Droughts

There are other issues central to the business and finance of production that I didn't travel far enough to experience, but through my work became very familiar with. One is the ability to handle producer-income droughts, and another is knowing whether or not you should leave your job.

If you're doing the work, busting your ass to create success, your checks can follow behind months, even years, after your work is done. Needlz shared that right after hooking up with his manager and getting a quick couple of placements, without factoring in the drought, he immediately began to upgrade his lifestyle. He learned a valuable lesson when he "moved to [an] apartment [and] thought it was gonna be all good, [but] was broke, [with] no placements for one and a half, two years; it happens a lot—cats think it's gonna be all good."

For those of you who'll grind into becoming a professional and for those of you already there, understand that you've got to be extra diligent with how you handle your money because—as DJ Khalil, with quite a few Platinum plaques under his belt, says—"You never know when your check is gonna come; *you just never know.*" Transmissions go into a coma, roofs leak, wisdom teeth need to be yanked, basements turn into pools, sons catch pneumonia, daughters want to throw sweet sixteens—when life happens, you've got to have some money stashed in preparation.

Let REO paint the picture with a little more detail:

> It's so hard to see your first check from music. I would sell beats locally to some … rapper; it would be a nice check, but it'd be like a bonus. You still had to have that money coming in to keep your rent paid. I think that even when I got my Beyoncé cut, *I didn't see any of my royalties for at least nine months … after that album came out. And I got the song to her people a year before that. So I had to wait a year before I even knew it was on the album, and then when the album actually came out, I had to wait another nine to ten months after that to see any money.*
>
> And so I think a lot of people get excited when they get a little check, and they wanna quit and say, "Screw you, I'm gonna make it!" Nah, man, you have to make sure that you've got enough money coming in to take care of it. And the problem, too, is that people sign pub[lishing] deals, and they get a lot of money up front, and they go, "Wow!" and they spend it all. They don't realize that the record company or publishing company is basically like a bank, they're giving you a loan; … *it pays them back first before it pays you, and I think a lot of people don't understand that.*
>
> When I signed my pub deal, I took less money up front so I could take [fewer] song commitments because I had already been schooled on that whole thing, and when I signed my deal, I still had a job. I just saved and saved and saved and kept working and working until I got myself enough of a cushion so that I could afford to take some time off. And just

in case I needed the money to get back on my feet, I had a cushion to save me. And luckily, I got the Beyoncé and Keyshia Cole cuts at the same time. I got a nice couple of producer fees and just saved my money, man. I think that's the key, you just gotta be real smart with your money, but it can be done.

The gaps between REO's checks when he got the ball rolling in his career are reality for someone who makes music for a living. You have to prepare for the drought. There will be good times, and there will be lean times. You don't want to be on your knees wishing you had good-time money in your lean times because you squandered dough on unnecessary crap during the good times. If you find yourself on the way to the strip club to make it rain, or the dealership to buy an expensive new car that'll lose half its value as soon as your tires touch the asphalt, hopefully you'll have my words reverberating throughout the cave of your mind.

The beauty of production creativity is not reflected in the production business. The business is hideous. It's ghastly. *It is not within your power to keep the faucet flowing smoothly at all times.* Obviously, there are plenty of producers who've mastered these hurdles and are doing damn well for themselves. But for every story of wealth and success, there are probably thirty of financial hardships. "[You] think it's gonna keep coming and coming, but the reality is, you're gonna have your hot years [and] a cold couple of years," warns Needlz. Managing producer droughts depends heavily on your ability to live within your means. Advises Focus,

> Then once you start to make the money, and your cost of living goes up, you kind of put yourself in a financial hole if that cost of living doesn't maintain. Since the last couple of years, I haven't been getting the same exact amount of music out, so now I have to pull back here and pull back there, just to make sure that I can keep maintaining for my family. There have been things that I've done and thought processes that I'm not so proud of.

To Quit or Not to Quit

To quit or not to quit the day job. I've heard arguments for both sides of the case for years, with the producers on the top telling younger producers to hold on to that day job until production can sustain you, and others saying there's no way to get it popping until you cut the safety rope. Not surprisingly, when I asked Needlz and DJ Khalil for their points of view, they were opposed. Needlz staunchly advocated holding on to the gig, while DJ Khalil said you have to cut the chains and step out there on faith. Both quit their jobs to take the leap.

According to DJ Khalil, there's no way to win while working a nine-to-five, coming home to make beats till four in the morning, only to return to work the next day. Regarding his own journey, he recalled,

> I just quit—"I'm [going to] do this full time, I'm [going to] be broke for a minute." Fresh out of college, ran up my credit card bill—[I] had to do what I had to do. No responsibilities, no house note, no kids, just my car.

> If you really want to do this for real, you gotta quit your job and suffer the consequences and ride it out. It's not easy. If you're gonna use your job as an excuse ... either you quit or you stay, but don't expect the same results. You have to bite the bullet and gut it out for a year. That's when the hustle comes in.

On the other hand, Needlz says there's nothing worse than making beats while you're dead broke. Worrying about when the power company is going to cut your lights off isn't conducive to being creative. He advises, "Please keep your job. I've had a lot of embarrassing broke days.... I don't recommend anybody quit their job ... because ... the game is getting smaller." I can attest to this fact. During the time this book was imagined and developed, I came face to face with the stress of my own "embarrassing broke days," when I had much more month than I had money. Being broke sits on your chest like a stack of barbell plates, stifling your creativity and focus with each wheezing, spastic breath. Being broke also creates a climate of desperation that makes it more difficult to deal with clients as people. Instead of sitting at a meeting with a man or woman, you imagine a giant, talking paid bill sitting across from you, or since you've been eating bologna and no-frills mayonnaise sandwiches for a week, picture a chatty six-foot steak. As you face the forked path with "job" on the left and "production" on the right, if quitting is the path you're prepared to walk, assess beforehand how well you can cope with the possibility of barbells of brokeness sitting on your chest.

Chuck Greene shared his point of view:

> I would never advise someone to quit their job. How'd you get this far? How were you able to buy your equipment? [There's] enough time in the day. Is it less sleep time? Absolutely. Once you quit your job, you have made the choice that [you are] all-in. Now look at the extra pressure that you put on [yourself], especially if you have people depending on you: ... rent, kid, girl. For you to quit, you gotta know you're taking a big gamble. Keep doing what you're doing, take down some sleep time, and let's land some big checks, something that gives you the ability to say, *I can quit now without putting a burden on my lifestyle.*

Focus, who also quit his job to make the dream work, doesn't advocate quitting your job in today's climate:

> I told myself I was gonna do this. I literally left my job, and I left in good standing. I made it to where it had to be an end-all-begin-all. So, when I left, I sold

> everything I had. I just had a bag of clothes, and I went out to the West Coast, and I was like, I'm not going back home; I gotta make it work here. And it took me some years....

> It's unfortunate, because ... this isn't one of those day and ages where you can just quit your job and say I'm gonna strive to be a producer, because if you don't hit it, then you're stuck....

> Continue to make the beats, try to get somebody's ear on it, somebody that you can trust, make sure they listen with an open mind and a good ear and give you the good criticism that you need.... Perfect what you're doing. Who knows, [the] next person that hears, it might be a placement.

There will never be unanimous agreement on this point, and you're going to have to judge your situation for yourself. A good point to keep in mind about some of the producers who did quit their jobs is that they made their decision early, fresh from college (or during), with a minimum of responsibilities. (Sound familiar? Remember that in the first chapter I spoke of how everything around you, especially the responsibilities you assume, will influence your ability to become successful at production?) I do agree that if you're going to quit, that's the way to go—do it before life makes its demands. Regardless of which route you choose, be prepared to handle the possible financial consequences.

To play devil's advocate, I want to add something that REO dropped on me regarding the importance of a job:

> Although everybody wants to quit their job and have all day and every day to make music, there is something really inspiring about having to work a job and still make music. You're at the job you hate and you're thinking about all the things you are gonna do when you get off. And you get home and it's like the most relaxing, relieving feeling. *"I can finally get to do what I want to do!"* And you just work.... You make the hottest stuff. You use your time a lot more efficiently.

> One of the things I ran into once I quit my job was realizing I had to be my own boss. Once the allure of getting to make music all day wears off, you kind of start saying to yourself, "Oh, I'm gonna work on that in a minute." "Yeah, I'm gonna finish that." "Yeah, I'll finish it later." But you sit down to watch a movie, you do this and you do that, next thing you know it's seven o'clock at night and *you haven't done a damn thing*. This is all depending on the kind of person you are, of course. For me, I have to set some sort of schedule with a list of things I want to accomplish by the end of the day or else nothing gets accomplished.

If you're not in a position to leave, use your current circumstances as motivation to make new circumstances. Use the desire to get out of your nine-to-five and aim it toward making hot music.

THE FINAL MIX

DJ Khalil, along with a few other professionals, mentioned that understanding and handling the business
is the most awful part of being a full-time producer.
Time and time again, I was told that one of the most
challenging obstacles on the road to success is gaining
a strong understanding of the business principles of
production—publishing, royalties, legal, copyrights,
licensing, sample clearances, etc. Mastering the business is as difficult as mastering the beats.

Focus confides,

> I hate it. I don't like dealing with it at all. I learned
> enough. There were two ways I learned it—[one,]
> by getting ran through, unfortunately, and two, by
> having great people in place. I have a great business
> manager from a firm that works for me and a great
> lawyer that works with me.

> So, when you get to the point where you are a
> Platinum producer or a Grammy-award-winning
> producer, you get to a standard ... and these lawyers
> and these business managers and even your personal
> manager [are] supposed to go after that. So, once I
> got there, it was pretty much coasting from there.

> But yeah, man, I hate the business, and I hate
> dealing with the greasy, slimy, dirty cats that do the
> business because they know how to put it in such a
> way that makes it feel so inviting, and then you sign
> it, and then you're stuck.... There has to be some
> kind of a loophole to get out of these situations
> that you get in.

The financial aspects of production cannot be ignored and may even play a role in shaping your creative process. I was fascinated to hear DJ Khalil reveal that the business side of things eventually changed the way he created. Through learning, he gained a stronger grasp of publishing, the equivalent of a squeegee across the cloudy glass of his business vision. With this vision, he realized how much potential income he was losing as a result of incorporating other people's works. He eventually decided to begin developing more original and interpolated works by taking piano lessons, learning more about music, and learning to work with a team to develop his own "moments in time" that he'd been capturing from sampling. The business and money forced him to evolve creatively so he could build a more prosperous future. You may one day find yourself in the same position.

Through other people's bad experiences, I've learned about the power of information in the record business. People who don't know are always at the mercy of people who do and can get it on paper. It's an absolute law of the entertainment business. People on top with knowledge or access to knowledge, an understanding of how processes work, where cash flow is generated, and access to attorneys, prey on those who have no knowledge of those things. It's like watching a pride of lions stalk an unsuspecting gazelle on the Discovery channel. The gazelle is standing there, oblivious, chewing grass, ignoring the details of the contract, and then wham! I've personally witnessed people set traps for unsuspecting victims and wait patiently with their arms crossed to see who walks into those traps. All of a sudden, you're at the mercy of somebody's nasty binding contract and legal process.

Says Focus,

> When it does come down to it, I've had situations where I've signed to people that I didn't do my research on, ... people I didn't do my homework on, and it put me in the situations that ... to me, could have been life threatening. I was just like "whoever wants to sign me, I'm ready to go," and I just did not do my research on the cats that were approaching me, and I got myself into a deal, a predicament, it was really hard for me to get out.... I never really wanted to be locked down into something that didn't feel like it was gonna make sense. And ... for some years in my life, I was. It was a scary experience, but you get through it.

Arm yourself with information; it's one of your strongest assets in the business. Google relentlessly: start with some of the terms you've seen in this chapter. Scour YouTube for answers. Ask questions endlessly like a five-year-old. Listen to podcasts, read articles, buy more books. And then begin the hunt for a great attorney. Not a real estate attorney or a family friend who used to be a divorce lawyer. Get an entertainment attorney—one with experience with labels and producers. Chuck Greene told me that an attorney is the first person to place on the team before you go hunting for a manager (by the way, when you're doing your thing properly, a manager will come hunting for you). The most important person in this business is the person who's got it on paper with an attorney standing by. Know thy business! You don't want to be one of those people doing an interview, telling the story of how fifteen years ago you were a part of a song that became a hit, and because you didn't know the publishing and copyright aspects of the situation, you missed out on several lifetimes of royalties. It happens.

You may be years away from applying some of these business concepts. If it's off in the distant future, stay focused on evolving your product, and for now, don't worry about the bread. You wouldn't believe how many successful producers told me they were giving beats away free until people started asking them what they charged. What mattered was the product. "It's not gonna be a direct check; it's a process and you build up your catalog and you have undeniable music, [then] you're gonna make money," DJ Khalil instructs. Read that quote again. All of you who swear you're going to make a quick buck to buy things you don't need, you're in the wrong place, buddy. This is a marathon, not a sprint. And even though production business principles may be off in the distant future and you're focused on your music, use this time to learn and understand so you're ahead of the curve when the time comes to put your knowledge to use.

> What I had to change was my understanding of people. Just being naïve and thinking that everybody thinks like you, ... everybody wants to do things the right way, it's just not like that. There are great people in the industry—don't get me wrong, it's not all evil—it's just [that they're] very few and far between. And I think a lot of the creative people, you know, on the come-up, everybody's hungry and stuff, they're like that, and they become gullible to other business-minded people who are like, "This person wants to get on so bad, I'm gonna offer them the worst deal ever."

> Even the *American Idol* stuff, it's just a real big sign showing you how much people want fame, because those contracts are ridiculous. But people sign them because they want to be famous, they want the glory, [they want] everyone to know their name, and they want to prove to their teachers, their boys, or their parents that they were wrong. —REO, the Soundkillers

LAW 19

First Impressions Count: Turn Your Mix and Equipment into Powerful Assets

My equipment is my cheat sheet. —Needlz

OBSERVATION

Although I did say that this book wasn't necessarily about the physical elements of production—software, hardware, and VSTs—there is one thing that I didn't do that I'm going to share with you so you'll avoid my mistake and save yourself some heartache.

I got killed by the crappy mix of my records, an aspect of production that hurts so many producers. Professionals can hear a poor mix from the first bar, and the total package is tainted as a result. Getting a hot beat with a bad mix is like getting a delicious, succulent steak served on a filthy trash-can lid. I used to whip out the digital mixer and randomly twist knobs with minimal understanding of what those knobs were supposed to do. I didn't know how to properly employ effects to add a professional touch. I was a waiter, repeatedly serving up that garbage-can steak

(I was probably serving more low-grade-beef burgers than steaks), but I never placed enough importance on the situation to solve the problem.

REALIZATION

I stood back and analyzed the situation some years ago. I concluded that making beats and mixing records are two different disciplines, two different sides of the same coin. Production is a creative process; you get in there and layer melodies on top of each other and get a funky groove going with your drum programming. You can have a natural disposition toward music and start making beats in no time. A few notes, a clap, and a heavy 808 can end up on the radio (mid-2000s crunk and snap were proof of this). But the mix, that's where the science comes in—the bookwork, the studying. The mix sits esoterically on the next rung of difficulty. It's a real barrier to entry, and a lot of producers, sadly, don't bother trying to climb over it. I was one of them.

A secret of music production is this: even if your track is average, if it sounds clean, crispy, and beautifully mixed, your effects are doing magnificent things, and those sounds slice out of the speakers like a katana blade, the nod factor rises substantially. You don't forget producers whose work sounds unusually crispy and professional, because it's so hard to achieve that level of polished sound.

Ric from Sweatbeatz says,

> Learn how to mix, or befriend an engineer. This
> doesn't mean devote your life to mixing instead
> of producing, but the quality of your mix is the
> first thing people notice when [you're] submitting
> tracks. It's just like your attire and appearance
> when you show up to a job interview; *your mix is
> the representation of how much you care about your
> work.* Even if you can't afford an engineer, at least
> gain knowledge about sound.

You need to be able to understand your mix and fa-
miliarize yourself with many of the technical aspects
of production. Understand frequencies, know where
instruments should sit in relation to other instruments, learn about compression and limiters. Learn
how to leave room in the mix for the artist and not
overcrowd your arrangements with sounds (something I was constantly guilty of). Master the ability
to make your 808s and kicks create crisp earthquakes
and aftershocks in rooms and cars. These skill sets
are where many producers come up short. Your production training regimen must include a strategy to
polish your mixing skills. YouTube is free, homeslice.
Sit there and let skilled engineers and producers show
you what they're doing to achieve a polished sound.

Know Your Setup As Well As You Know Yourself

Also, whatever tools you work with in your studio—
know them intimately. "Master your equipment!

Read manuals!" says Needlz. He's absolutely right. His deep knowledge of his equipment gives him an edge and he's learned to do things the average producer hasn't. This strategy improves his workflow and boosts his creativity.

Advises REO,

> I think one of the most important things you could ever do is *spend so much time with your equipment that you learn all of its mistakes.* Because whenever you get a new piece of gear, and you're trying to be creative, and you don't know how to make it do what you want to do in your head, that always stunts your process.

> So, once you learn, like, okay, it's doing that, I know how to fix that..., I think that is a huge deal with making music. Because you've gotta learn how to get through it. I definitely feel like that equipment stuff is one of the top ones because when you're in a situation where you're in the studio, and you're with the ... top songwriter and you need to perform, you need to be able to make it do what it do. *Nothing is worse than being in the room and you don't know your stuff.*

You have to be in a position to make your equipment do whatever you need it to do. You have to know your equipment's strengths and weaknesses just as well as you know your own. Be familiar with how your equipment processes sound, how you need to compensate for things in the mixes, which patches and sounds are strong and which are weak, and more.

With mastery of your equipment, you'll open a new lane of creative maneuverability. Think about the pro sports legends; they have the fundamentals down so well they don't have to think about them. They can focus purely on creating in the moment because they've already been through thousands of hours mastering the fundamentals. Mastery over your setup gives you the same advantage.

THE FINAL MIX

Take a few weeks at a time (remember those breaks we spoke of) and learn how to proficiently mix your records and tracks. You might not have the bread to pay engineers to mix every beat, so take a little time and make it a part of your arsenal.

There's nothing new or groundbreaking about my warning you about your mix. I'm just explaining its power as both a producer and a person who's sifted through beats looking for tracks to shop. It's an attention-commanding part of your production. My challenge to you is this: will you read this and just continue on your way? Or will you take a break from your beats and invest two, three, or four weeks into *just* mixing? Will you go so far as to hunt down a master engineer and pay him to teach you how to make your tracks bang? You could evolve significantly for what someone would pay for a pair or two of fly kicks. There are plenty of skilled engineers out there with time to teach.

LAW 20

Listen, Learn, Evolve: Develop a Palette for Good Music to Make Good Music

OBSERVATION

I'm glad to say that during my time producing, I managed to have a few moments of clarity and make a few smart decisions. I've been fortunate enough to be utterly fascinated by *all music*. I can be in the condiment aisle at the grocery store, hear something funky like an old Tears for Fears record coming from the speakers, freeze while in mid-reach for Jif peanut butter, process, screw up my face, and jam out. As a kid, I used to pause *Sonic the Hedgehog 2* just to listen to the music that still played. I still have all the music from those games floating in the back of my mind, twenty years later (a lot of the music from Sonic sounds like Neptunes beats to me). I sit in the dark and listen to music; I don't need any additional stimulation besides the glorious chords, instrument sounds, and melodies that I'm hearing.

I can thank my father for all of this; the apple doesn't fall far, and it's from him that I got the ability to embrace almost every genre. I grew up hearing funk, jazz, blues, progressive rock, and New Age. And although I was strictly hip-hop through my teens, I returned to my diverse essence as I hit my twenties. I'm fascinated by the fact that all music, including all of those amazing chord combinations, derives from the same twelve tones. The same incredible melody or chord progression can live in a hip-hop beat, jazz record, New Age groove, or '80s-hair-band ballad. Sampling is proof of that. So, if you're a producer, how could you not love it all? Everything boils down to the same common elements.

Pink Floyd, David Axelrod, Mandrill, Quincy Jones, Ten Wheel Drive, Rotary Connection, Jimi Hendrix, Metallica, Joe Sample, Bob James, Lalo Schifrin, The Stylistics, Billy Paul, Renaissance, Steely Dan, Genesis, Yes, King Crimson, The Beatles, Nirvana, The Dramatics, C.P.E. Bach, The Dells, Foo Fighters, Chick Corea, Mahavishnu Orchestra, Herbie Hancock, David Ruffin, Lamont Dozier, Sade, Kyoto Jazz Massive, Antonio Vivaldi, Bjork, Bob Marley, Barrington Levy, Johnny Pate, Ennio Morricone, Jerry Butler, The Persuaders, Nine Inch Nails, Parliament, Queens of the Stone Age, Daft Punk, Johannes Brahms, Lee Ritenour, Marvin Gaye, Stevie Wonder—I could make this chapter go on forever with incredible artists who inspire me.

There's something magical about artists who just have it—melodies that whisper to your soul, bass lines that act as snake charmers to your body, and musical phrases that survive in your memory no matter the number of decades that pass, the amount of alcohol ingested, or the type of drugs consumed. I've always wondered what it is that makes these artists and songs so timeless, that gives them so much power over us. I knew I would give myself some sort of advantage by embracing, listening to, and appreciating as many forms of music as I could. So I studied. I absorbed. I tried to make myself aware. I believe to this day that listening was an integral part of my ability to at least construct original material despite the whole process being so alien.

Be a fan of incredible music and a student of the kind of music that survives decades. Comprehend what you're listening to. Understand the use of different instruments and sounds; process how they maneuver throughout the song, how instruments combine, harmonize, and fuse into music. Pinpoint features of incredible music: the uniqueness of Barry White's strings; the distinctive snap of the snare in Al Green's records; the unbelievable arrangements that connect to form legendary Bob James songs; the evocative songwriting of Kurt Cobain. Seek to understand how those elements unite to create amazing moments in time.

Watch a band lay down records. Immerse yourself in the creation process and examine it from multiple angles. And arm yourself with as much music theory as possible. You'll open a whole new creative world in which you can make new compositions. Strive to make the kind of music that, several years from now, some young producer will want to sample.

As time passes, I wonder if new producers are aware of all the great music that has come before them. I've missed much, but by using sampling as a time machine to the past, I've backtracked to a lot of incredible jazz, soul, rock, and everything in between. One of my favorite archeological discoveries came through a 9th Wonder–produced Ludacris song that unearthed a Brazilian jazz artist named Arthur Verocai. Verocai composes unbelievable Bossa Nova jazz music. I searched for four months and finally paid thirty bucks for a low-fi, rare CD of his amazing self-titled album.

Study the compositions, the chord progressions, and the sounds. To this day, Pink Floyd has some of the most beautiful synths I've ever heard, and that was forty years ago, and let's not even talk about the mix on their records. Understand the brilliance of producers like Isaac Hayes, Robin Millar, Lamont Dozier, Trevor Horn, Nellee Hooper, and Dr. Luke.

Know that your musical palette may be much more diverse than you are aware of. Some of you know this, and this is good, but for those of you who know only a certain style of music, realize that the genres we young people enjoy today have their roots in every other genre on earth. If you're listening to West Coast–based productions, you're also a fan of Parliament, the Ohio Players, Bootsy Collins, and an entire era of funk records. If you love Jay-Z's first album, then you're a jazz fan and may be interested in Lonnie Liston Smith, Ahmad Jamal, and Marcus Miller. If you're vibing out to Daft Punk, there's jazz and soul behind those cats. Many popular records have their roots in other genres, especially through sampling. Expand the boundaries of your musical mind, make them vast—go back to the classics, process, investigate, and use what you learn to evolve as a creator. The styles change—one era of music dies and another is born in its place—but great music is great music, regardless of time. Whether it's from 1969 or 1999, you can extract a few quantifiable items that make a record amazing. Your job as a producer is to incorporate these elements of greatness into your music so people are listening to what you've done twenty years from now (and you can reap that long-term publishing). Studying and appreciating will help you do this.

THE FINAL MIX

Are you familiar with all of the artists I've mentioned in this chapter? If you are, then I'm impressed. But I speculate that many of you, especially my millennial readers, may not know these musicians and producers. If you couldn't identify any of those names, I hope you didn't intend to move on to the next chapter without taking a moment to Google some of them. Did you make a point to figure out what act Robin Millar is behind that you can regularly hear on the radio twenty-five years later? Did you even bother checking out Bob James or Steely Dan? If not, go and immerse yourself in different genres of music and seek to understand what makes the great, great.

> Everybody has opinions about what's amazing, what's classic, what's this and that, and who is the greatest to ever do it, but I think you should just find out who your favorites are and study them. Study what makes them stand out from everyone else or what about [their music] makes it dope to you. Once you learn those things, interpret that in your own way and see what happens. Then you can start asking yourself, "What would you do differently, or how can you take these ideas and expand upon them?"

> I think that listening is a really, really big deal. Take the time to just sit and listen like a student. Take notes if you have to. Even if I don't make anything for a week, I'm always listening, always learning, always thinking about how I can make things better, and I think that when I sit down to create again, I've already gotten better because I've mapped out my next moves. —REO, the Soundkillers

LAW 21

Learn Sensei's Secrets: Find a Master, Visit His Dojo, Study His Technique

OBSERVATION

I remember two instances when, after realizing how much I could evolve as a creator of music, I made a point to watch somebody very talented make beats. The first instance was maybe sometime in 2004 and, because I was only a few months into making beats, was probably one of the smartest things I ever did. I was fresh out of college, blessed with a brand new MPC1000 for a graduation present. The same producer I had met a few years before as a freshman, Eddie Bronco, was in Chicago, where I landed after college. He hooked me up with the producer who, if you remember, was playing those dope songs that influenced me to wrongly handcuff my own beats. I was already a huge fan of this guy's work, and I finally caught him standing still for a moment and drove into the suburbs of south Chicago to link up.

I arrived at his home, a neat but unassuming ranch house with a big green lawn, and as I entered, he led me down into his basement/laundry room/studio. Amid the huge white washing set and piles of clothes were an MPC2000, a boombox, and his vinyl collection, sloppily strewn about the room as if a mild hurricane had whirled through a record store. My eyes wandered around the small space in frantic search for the rest of his equipment because, surely, the beats I heard weren't coming out of *this* room with only *that* stuff.

Unable to locate whatever extra equipment I thought he had to be using, I unfolded my list of his beats. "Okay bruh, show me how you made this one, this one, and this one." He proceeded to fire up his equipment, like a pilot readies a helicopter, and began exposing the secret blueprints and architecture for all his beats. It was like being at a magic show. He taunted me with the original samples, heightening the performance before revealing his intricate chops, clever drum programming, and crafty EQ and effects tricks. He even cut a few samples right then as I stood there watching his hands whir around the buttons of the MPC—recording, slicing, trimming, and assigning so fast his fingers looked like the wings of a hummingbird in midflight. As if I were a shocked cartoon character, my jaw fell to the floor, a puddle of drool amassing before me. *I could not believe what I was watching.* I had no idea you could do what he was doing on an MPC. In my first months of music production, I felt like a hairy caveman, marveling after just inventing the wheel, while this guy zoomed by me laughing hysterically in a Porsche. His technique was as dope as his beats, and I understood why he sounded like he did. That day, he was the No I.D. to my Kanye West.

That decision to sit and watch somebody compose put a stick of dynamite at the iron gate of my own imagination. I realized that it's one thing to hear a good beat, but it's a different galaxy to sit and watch the actual creation of it. I also realized the importance of knowing your equipment like the back of your hand. This cat knew his setup and could make it do whatever he wanted. He expanded the potential of the MPC's basic EQ and effects features, pulling out techniques I didn't know one could do. It's similar to the experience the social networking generation gets from watching other producers on YouTube today, but there's nothing like being present as fantastic works are created in front of you. Nothing. I absolutely recommend that you find some producers who are light years ahead of you and be in their presence as they create. I learned a lot of valuable lessons that day, and they allowed me to skyrocket my ability to cut and arrange samples.

The second time I visited a superior producer's studio and blew my mind was years later in Atlanta. I linked up with a producer named DJ Speedy when he was doing a lot of good work, particularly with Young Jeezy and CTE Records. This was probably about three years into my journey, sometime in 2007, and around the time I was trying to demystify original production and music theory. I made the drive deep into the eastern side of Atlanta, a good thirty-five to forty minutes away, and by the time I left Speedy's studio, I was a different beatmaker.

I walked into his studio and discovered that he was a hardware man to the core. The room contained a neatly arranged but complex spiderweb of keyboards, audio cables, and equipment, a setup that mirrored the bridge of the Starship Enterprise more than a producer's studio. I had the opportunity to listen to his volume of work, which shook me because not only was his music of substantial quality, but he was also ridiculously prolific. He scrolled through his own beats in an iTunes playlist for what seemed like a half-hour. Incredulous, I stared at the screen, wondering where in God's name the bottom of his playlist was.

I realized I had a hell of a journey in front of me, in terms of both evolving my product and developing a meaty catalog. I heard how properly mixed 808 drums hit, and I heard what went into creating those distinct Southern sounds. I heard the artist he was working with. It was my cold-water-on-the-face moment, and I sadly dragged myself back to my car, heartbroken as a child who was eating his ice cream cone, licked too hard, and knocked a scoop off the side. In another moment of proper thinking, I put myself in a position to better see what it was *really* going to take to win. And after I passed through my quick depression, the experience lit a firestorm of desire in me, and I couldn't wait to get home and get to work.

You must put yourself in these kinds of positions. Some of my biggest creative leaps came after witnessing firsthand someone else's incredible talent and production process. Afterward, I would race home to try to incorporate what I'd learned before it slipped through a grate in my memory and was lost forever. *Find someone whose sound baffles you, and watch him craft music.* Don't go to someone who is as good as you. Oh no. Find someone who makes you stare at the speaker and cock your head to the side like a confused puppy. You want to sit in with that guy. Few things will wake you up like sitting in a session with a ridiculously talented producer, especially one who's still on his way up, because you then realize that *that* person, who's got you sitting there with your mug scrunched up with the screw-face, is sending out music to the same places you are. It's time to get your game up, and this is the perfect method to do so.

THE FINAL MIX

This is not a chapter for reflection; this is a chapter for action. *Do not let six months pass* and you haven't done this. Find that immensely talented producer, buddy up, and get to his studio. (Are you that immensely talented producer? Pass on what you know!) I promise you, if you focus and absorb, the experience will force creative growth. Make a habit out of it.

You want to know how Jimi Hendrix got so damn good at playing the guitar, to the point where he holds the title as the most gifted guitar player to ever live (not to mention he was playing it backward because he was left-handed)? Everywhere he went, as he traveled on the road playing in bands, he asked talented guitarists who were masters of their craft to teach him some licks.

To conclude, check what Focus had to say about sitting and watching the ultimate mentor, Dr. Dre:

> I loved watching him mix a record; it's a definite craft that he's perfected—it's where he shows ... the drive [to be a] perfectionist. Like, he shows the reason why it has to sound a certain way when he starts to mix, and that was pretty much the highlight and the best part of working for Aftermath....
>
> Being able to be around when he was mixing records for, like, Em and 50 and Jay-Z and hearing

the records in the raw and then hearing them after
he was finished and seeing the little subtleties that
he would put in there that made a difference to the
trained ear—he is an amazing producer, and it was
an honor just to be around that.

Part 5: Conclusion

LAW 22

Know Thyself: Assess You—If You're Not Right, Nothing Will Be

This chapter is short, but don't be fooled by its length. I have some key questions for you: Who are you? Do you know yourself? Do you know yourself well? I ask because you need to know whether you're built for this business. *Easily* becoming a producer is an extremely rare occurrence (if it happens at all). For most, this production game is similar to a gauntlet. As you jog through it, life circumstances, responsibilities, the entertainment business, your own self (hence this book), and your family stand on both sides with clubs, rocks, bats, and hockey sticks to beat you with.

It can come from anywhere. "Even my family?" you ask. Especially your family! Once-supportive husbands grow increasingly uncomfortable with wives producing in the studio with strange men at all hours of the night. Fathers, yesterday happy to see you pursue something cool they never got to, today rain lectures about putting away foolish pursuits, buckling down, and being responsible for your family. Sweet girlfriends become as sour as lemons over the time a boyfriend's fingers spend tickling ivory instead of tickling them. Enthusiastic mothers, once encouraging, tire of hearing their friends discuss the promotions won and degrees attained by their children. "Oh Jimmy? Well, he's doing his music thing, looking for his break," she says, disappointment dripping from each syllable. The years will go on. Success may not be visible to your loved ones. Out of what they see as love and the hope of saving you from pain and disappointment, they may come like thieves in the night to steal your drive and enthusiasm. When these forces come for you, whether they are close to home or not, will you be strong enough to be battered while you run the gauntlet?

Know thyself. Are you lazy? Are you nervous about dealing with thugs and paper gangsters? Do you like sleep? Do you like having a high credit score? Do you like living by yourself? Are you sensitive? How long can you be broke? Do you lose interest quickly? How do you feel about working with scum? Are you humble?

You may be in the wrong place. As you answer these questions, be honest with yourself. There's nobody here but you. You know that process of self-discovery I discussed at the beginning of the book, that period when I sought to eliminate the many negative emotions, habits, and self-made obstacles within? You may need to do a self-purge. It's cool, because that's the beauty of being human—you get to change at any moment you *decide* to.

Are you passionate? Are you patient? Are you dedicated? Do you know true persistence? Are you fueled by a desire to be the best? Are you thick-skinned? Do you know no defeat? Are you intelligent in mind and heart? Are you willing to take a step back to take two steps forward? Are you a chameleon, able to deal with all types of people? Do you believe in continuous education? Are you never satisfied? Then you have a place here.

Jay-Z, in his song "December 4th," rapped a clever line about a man being defined when his well runs dry. I always thought it was a deep line, but I neglected to realize its truth in my own life when it was my time to define myself in the middle of my own droughts. Felisha Booker liked to remind me during my challenging times, "Who are you when the shit looks bad?" Years later, I can still hear her question echoing in my mind. It's a question I pass on to you, because it's applicable and relevant to any worthwhile dream or pursuit. While watching me come into my own droughts several times, she reminded me that doing what you want to do and doing what you love to do can be extremely difficult. That's why chasing dreams is something done only by the few; it's easier to melt into what's easy and available, into what you see right before your eyes instead of what is far in the distance of your vision.

I've always been sensitive about those who irresponsibly shoot off the phrase "follow your dreams" like some kid who's found his older brother's BB gun in the back of the closet. Because dream-following can have heavy costs. It should be, "Become strong enough to follow your dreams. Then follow them." Becoming who you're supposed to be can be a hard thing to accomplish. And it's essential to accept that truth. You need that acceptance as a producer. You don't have to like it, but the sooner you can accept that the path you've chosen can sometimes feel like pushing a boulder up a hill covered in motor oil while you're wearing skates, the sooner you can refocus on what you came to accomplish.

You will struggle through your own droughts to find success. But who are you when it's bad, when the checking account has a negative balance, when the gas gets cut off, when your parents tell you to give up these foolish pursuits and get a job or you're cut off, when someone breaks into your studio and steals all of your hard drives and equipment, when you live in a tiny one-bedroom in the ragged part of town because you can't afford anything else, when you're knee-deep in a bad contractual agreement, when the debt is piling into an avalanche rushing to bury you alive, when your dinner choice is constantly between beef or chicken, but not actual beef or chicken, beef or chicken Ramen noodles?

See, it's easy to keep your spirits high and grind with a huge grin on your face when everything's okay. But what kind of person are you when it hits the fan? Felisha's question rings with truth: time and time again, the successful producers interviewed for this book gave me their "shit hit the fan" moments. They've all had times of drought, when they were praying for water. But what sets successful producers apart is that instead of dropping to their knees and identifying with the challenges around them, instead of curling up in the fetal position and giving power to the idea of just giving up, they accepted that this was the price to pay for their dreams, for excellence, for leaving an identifiable mark on the world of music, and they dragged themselves forward to achieve. Instead of giving those challenges power, they kept their minds focused on their visions, on what they were going to find a way to accomplish. Who are we when the world tests us? If you seek to accomplish something wonderful, then tested you will be.

I'm grateful for getting a glimpse into the lives of these Platinum-plus and Grammy-winning producers to remind me of this fact. When the rains of positivity and comfort stop falling in my own life and it's drought time, I'll have their words ringing in the back of my head as I accept the fact that this is what it costs to be who I'm supposed to be, to maximize my potential. And I'll pick myself up from my knees and keep moving forward toward my goals. And so will you.

THE FINAL MIX

Remember, your success relies *mostly* on what you have bouncing around in that brain of yours (I wanted to say *entirely*, but the truth is, you'll need people to help you get where you want to go, and you'll need luck). But you have to make sure you stay out of your own way. What do I mean by that? Many times producers arrest their own development by letting things like pride and ego cloud their judgment. When you get to thinking that you're too hot to do certain things you need to do, that you're above working with certain people who could be of service to you, that the production world owes you something, that A&Rs should be blowing up your phone, you may be headed for trouble.

Dow reflects,

> The other thing that kills off a lot of cats is just pride, from you getting your first hit or you getting your first little placement, you're popping, now you ain't messing with nobody no more, you're the [dude]. Then you start seeing that paper slow up and try to get back to these cats you were messing with before and they're not f*cking with you. Because your pride got in the way and you weren't humble

enough to just accept your blessings for what they were, *so even when shit does happen, or you do need to try to go in different avenues, you can still go through those doors.*

As you seek to know yourself, learn to stay out of your own way. Strive to remain humble and hungry at all times (easier said than done). Even if you're experiencing some success, maintain the mindset that you're at the bottom and you've got to fight just as you did from day one.

REO also had something to say regarding this issue of being able to maintain one's humble nature:

I think it's difficult to stay humble when you've gotten so many no's. I think that that's what happens a lot of times to people: [you hear], "No, no, no, no, no," and when you finally get a yes, you're like, "Screw you!" to everyone, and I feel like it's hard to not be bitter. It takes a strong person to turn around and say, "Hey, that's the game, that's the way it is, it wasn't time, it is now," and just take it with a grain of salt and enjoy it while it's there. And when it's not, when the high is coming down, you didn't step on any heads or mess anybody over, so then people still rock with you.

Nobody owes you anything in the music business. Even the hottest producers of the moment can be left behind in the dust in no time, so keep that in mind if you ever catch yourself swimming in a sea of pride. The fairly talented producer who's willing to view himself as always fighting from the bottom, who's open to any and all, who's humble, grateful, and focused on getting it, *he can outpace you.* While you're resting on your laurels, letting your ego do the thinking, the other guy has a more powerful mind-set, and his hustle is stronger for it. Eventually, his hustle will allow him to capitalize on opportunities you think you're too good for.

Be careful how you deal with people, be mindful of what opportunities you dismiss, and be aware of the vibe you put out when doing business. I see so many beatmakers who are nonchalant, nasty, forgetful, dismissive, and impatient, and they destroy opportunities without even knowing it. They haven't run an honest inventory of themselves, like you're about to do after reading this chapter. That's who they are as people, and who you are as a person is who you are as a producer. I've been on the receiving end of these attitudes, and after that, those producers don't hear from me anymore.

Stay out of your own way. The only thing that can stop you from becoming who you're supposed to be is you. This is something I've learned the hard way. It's so true it's scary.

LAW 23

Uncomfortable Comfort: Escape the Clutches of Your Comfort Zone

Comfort is a joy of life. We work so hard to arrange things in our lives, dedicating years to studying, earning, failing, loving, and living so we can land perfectly in a place of comfort. However, for those who have destinies to manifest and purposes to fulfill, the comfort of our circumstances and the comfort zones we shelter ourselves within are the enemies of our success.

I have come to believe that one cannot be constantly comfortable if one seeks higher levels of success. I told you how, as a beatmaker, I was adamant about improving certain areas of my producer situation, but *under my own terms*. I was way too comfortable in my own room, night after night, with my music and the cozy circumstances I created for myself. I hadn't developed the strength to shake myself from my own comfort zone, and it held me back, as you can tell. If you are constantly comfortable, you will never force yourself to take the actions you need to, to the detriment of your progress as a producer.

Around the time I began writing this book, I began to learn about the power gained from being able to leave your comfort zone. I've been blessed with family members and bosses who've ripped me from my zone and forced considerable growth. That's the blessing you receive when you leave familiar territory: you expand to new levels. And you're standing there looking at yourself in the mirror of self-awareness, confused, trying to recognize this new person with these new abilities. It's a beautiful experience, and although my growth applied to professional and career moves more than to making beats, you can give yourself the same gift as creators of music.

CONQUERING THE FEAR OUTSIDE OF YOUR COMFORT ZONE

I remember coming across a couple of Will Smith interviews some years back. Will's one of my favorite stars, and among a special brand of entertainer because he's excelled in so many disciplines and roles: music creator, TV star, film star, producer, etc. Will dropped some of the most powerful and inspirational information I've ever heard. He said he hates being scared of something. He hates the feeling of fear. So he attacks what he fears until it is known and conquered and no longer a fear. He's willing to step outside of his comfort zone, into the unknown, to cancel out something that's holding

him back. In the same fashion, you have to attack
your fears, which keep you safely cocooned in your
career comfort zone. If you look in your own soul
and know that you have more to grow, more you
could be doing to become, you must start making
yourself uncomfortable and attacking those fears so
you can expand. Attack the things that hold you
back. Gain the gift of looking at yourself in disbelief as you demonstrate new abilities that, just
months before, you thought you didn't have.

Remember what Dow said: "All producers are just
comfortable, they're comfortable in the studio just
making stuff." If you want to make a career out of
this, you can't afford to be comfortable on the way
up. You have to continuously stretch yourself to be a
part of what Tha Bizness is a part of, to keep pushing the boundaries of your skill and reach new levels
of success. Once your success earns you material
comfort—your upfront fees and publishing have allowed you to upgrade your lifestyle and provide won-
derfully for your family—comfort is still an enemy
to the producer. As the sound of music evolves, and
new classes of beatmakers move into the workforce
daily, you must remain diligent and uncomfortable
so you don't find yourself obsolete. You'll need to
perform a balancing act: enjoying and appreciating
the blessings of your success without being tranquil-
ized by them. A hard thing to do, yes, I know. But

walking that fine line while blocking the powerful sedative that comfort pumps into your bloodstream is essential to building a long-term career in production. Don't give in to the part of yourself that wants you to be comfortable with where you are. You have more to become.

Take risks. Do the unordinary. Meet new people. Put yourself in new circumstances and situations. Try new styles of music. Work with new artists. Work out of new studios. Avoid safe, habitual routines. Examine and avoid the circumstances, the metaphorical snooze buttons, which may have you a little too relaxed, a little too comfortable with your situation. Attack your fears on the other side of comfort; keep your mind trained on growth and expansion.

LAW 24

Preparation, Meet Opportunity: Being Ready Means You Don't Waste Time Getting Ready

OBSERVATION

Let me tell you about one of the things I love about living. This particular thing helps to keep me excited; it's the electric-eel-filled moat that surrounds my thought castle and keeps the armies of depression and despair from storming my mind. *You never know when a blessing or opportunity will present itself.* You could be obscured in total darkness, you couldn't even imagine how you'll make a way, and a solution will swing open like a door, with the shining light of opportunity, of hope and possibility, cleaving right through the darkness. You didn't anticipate the blessing, but it's there, jumping out, happily shocking you shitless like loved ones hiding behind a kitchen counter at a surprise party. "Oh my God, I can't believe this worked out!" or, "How the hell did I get the lead single!" you think to yourself. We never know when beautiful blessings or opportunities will come waltzing merrily into our lives. But when they do, you better damn well be prepared to take advantage of them.

Several years ago, I was grocery shopping at my local Kroger on the southwest side of Atlanta. As clear as day, I remember turning the aisle and, standing in front of me with his lady, shopping for groceries, was none other than the yellow-skinned King of the South, T.I. No security, no gaggle of homies, just Tip and his lady grabbing groceries in the middle of the night, just like me. After unlocking my frozen body, then somehow stopping myself from turning into a twelve-year-old girl and rushing T.I. for an autograph, I nodded nonchalantly, feigning coolness, and continued to shop. I perused the aisles some more, and when my opportunity came, I mustered up the courage to tell him that I was a big fan of his music, I loved what he did as an artist, and *I looked forward to getting him some beats one day*. I "look forward" was what I said.

REALIZATION

I didn't have any beats with me. Who knows what could have happened if I'd had a disc and he'd been in a receptive mood? He could've played it in the car on the way to take his groceries home, or on the way to the studio, and jammed the brakes, skidding over to the side of the road, to exclaim, "Sweet Mother of Jesus! This MayDay is a damn musical genius!"

Okay, I'm dreaming, but hey, you never know. Opportunities in this game come from *out of nowhere!* On Monday, you're sitting there ravaged by rotten circumstances, deciding between food in your belly and electricity in your outlets, and on Tuesday, someone can call you to say you've got a single and completely change your life.

You have to be prepared for those calls and those e-mails and those meetings and those chance run-ins at Kroger in the middle of the night. You do this by making sure that your music is up to par, your mixes are up to par, you're professional, and you have music with you at all times—especially when you live in a city like Atlanta and a major artist might pull up to the gas pump next to you and ask, "What's happenin', partnah?" People with their homing beacons locked on success stay prepared: in their gut they know that everything serves their evolution. They *expect* opportunity to knock at any moment. Always keeping good music on hand is just the physical manifestation of that expectation of success.

I would suggest that in addition to riding around with a CD of your well-produced and well-mixed music, you keep thumb drives with you (you should get them branded). Load them with your tracks, contact information, and a link to your Web presence—all the essentials. (Make sure that you have some sort of Web presence—a SoundCloud page, Bandcamp,

Don't Make Beats Like Me

or custom website—and that you can be reached.)
Even today, I still run into producers with no Web
presence. Who does that! Some producers fear that
by putting their music online, they will be robbed or
copied. They might be. I've advised these producers
that such a fear should not prevent them from having
some kind of presence online, and to imagine their
beats as eggs. Receivers of this advice scrunch their
foreheads in confusion. I explain that some of the
eggs will be damaged during shipping to the grocery
store. It may have been a lovely egg, but you copyright what you can, and you make sure your chickens
can keep making more eggs so you don't lose sleep
over the one or two that go missing.

Also, keep your presentation in mind when soliciting music. People are bombarded with thousands of
discs at hundreds of events, so the first hurdle to get
over is how to present your material to get a listen. I
was one of the cats with his contact info scribbled on
a blank disc with a Sharpie. Meanwhile, my homies
from Sweatbeatz Productions developed a logo,
printed jewel-case inserts and disc covers, and when
possible, personalized the material for the receiving
party—an impeccable presentation. Will all music
professionals care how they receive their music?
Nope. Will every exec or manager care if your info is
printed neatly or scribbled on? Nope. Will your beautifully designed artwork and presentation make some

young intern zero in on your disc amid the hundreds in the pile? Not necessarily. But there's no negative to having a polished, professional presentation. Show people that you mean business, that they can trust investing their money in you.

When you've prepared properly for Lady Luck— you've filled the room with the soothing sounds of light jazz, poured two glasses of sweet red wine, dimmed the lights to the appropriate level of sexy— Lady Luck walks in and looks at your preparation, and her inviting eyes tell you she's ready. Ric from Sweatbeatz believes in this philosophy:

> Get lucky! Sometimes it's not about the overt things you do; sometimes it's about you being in the right place at the right time. I don't mean luck like winning the lottery. [It's] setting yourself up to receive your blessing. Going to industry events, noticing [what] platforms A&Rs speak about on Twitter, having your most updated beat CD/USB on you whenever you go out. When some unexpected opportunity is presented, at least you have your goods and *mind right* to get your music in the right hands.

"Right place, right time" is something I've seen play out many times when it comes to producers. But as Ric says, all the work you've done beforehand puts you in a position to get lucky more often than not because you're prepared for the blessing. As movie mogul Samuel Goldwyn put it, "The harder I work, the luckier I get."

THE FINAL MIX

I'd like to share a brief thought on professionalism as it relates to preparation. I know beats are flying around the world via e-mail nowadays. For God's sake, please put your contact information in the MP3 file *and* encode the ID3 tags on your files so the correct information pops up when the disc is inserted into people's media players. In all my time working with producers, the only thing that's made me want to be physically violent toward people is receiving an e-mail with a sloppy introduction, the writing skills of a toddler, and three or four beats titled "Club Joint 1," "Club Joint 2," "Club Joint 3." At my busiest at Dynamic Producer, I had several hundred files going in different places on my computer. Like most busy people who are getting beats, I wasn't fishing through anything to find out where I got "Club Joint 3."

Put your name and song title in the file name for quick identification (and send an MP3, not one of those damn WMA files). Show people that you care. And be professional in your written correspondences. "Yo. Dis John Doe Beats. Listen to my beat" does not relay the fact that you care about your career. Several times, unsuspecting producers have gotten a nasty response from me calling them out on their lack of professionalism. And they can't even say anything because they know I'm right. So represent yourself as a business, man.

Fix your mind on the possible blessings headed your way. Sharpen your creative sword before they come. Be prepared when they strike. And get lucky!

OUTRO

"Man, I don't want to be doing music when I'm forty." Why not? If this is what you love to do, I don't understand. What else would you want to do? —Hen, Tha Bizness

Every time they fly us out somewhere to go work, we always look at the other people at the airport, these guys in business suits with the super-tight necktie, just looking hella uncomfortable and frustrated and they hate where they're going. But to us, it's another adventure; we're ready to go! —Dow, Tha Bizness

VICTORY REDEFINED

How do *you* define success? What is victory for a producer? Along with never stepping back and envisioning what I wanted from this art, I never thought about what victory meant for MayDay. I just assumed that you had to be this guy who worked with major artists and labels and was famous and respected. I was blinded by some of the false imagery of hip-hop victory: gaudy Jesus pieces, untold fortune, fame, expensive cars with bad gas mileage, an army of sex-thirsty groupies, exclusive parties, overpriced cocktails spilled on suede VIP couches. That's what

I assumed victory as a music maker was supposed to look like.

But I've learned that for many who do this for a living, who have matured and have families to provide for, that's not really what it is. That's not everyone's vision of victory. J-Thrill, a talented cat who works with DJ Khalil's camp of super-creative producers, said something interesting to me years ago: "It's a blessing to be able to do music and make $40,000 a year—we're not all going to be Timbaland and Kanye West." That's a monstrous statement that shines a sobering light of reality. It may not be what a lot of us want to hear, but it's the truth. Even though our faces won't all be on magazine covers, it's important to realize that the true blessing lies in being able to do this thing you love, make a good living, and take care of yourself and your family from the work you do.

Some of you may have been brainwashed like me, blinded with the assumption that the goal should be obtaining fortune and fame. There's nothing wrong with that dream, but understand what the real blessing is. To wake up in the morning, head to your studio, fire up your equipment, and make music—for a living—is a real blessing. Fortune or fame or anything of that nature is sweet icing on an already delicious cake.

There are some very successful producers you've never seen and whose names you don't know who excel at their craft, do what they love, and more than sufficiently feed their families. They aren't the subject of magazine spreads and in-depth interviews. They could be standing behind you in the grocery store, and you wouldn't have a clue. But they make a living making music that they love and are living their dream. That's success to me!

When I was a snot-nosed twenty-three-year-old, I never took into account the beauty of earning a living from your talent and passion. I was conditioned for mediocrity: earn a respectable degree, get a job that looks good on paper whether you love it or not, keep your head down, slave away in your cubicle, wear your jeans and Hawaiian-themed shirt on dress-down Fridays, and make the owners and shareholders rich. Dow says,

> Our main thing is, you're successful because you can wake up every day and do what you want to do. And you do that at such a good level that other people see value in that and pay you for that. So, what else is there really to ask for?

Dow's statement echoes my redefined version of victory—serving the world with your talents, talents you've polished so well that you earn a nice living from them. What else can you possibly ask for?

Take the idea of chasing money off the table. Time and time again, these top cats have revealed to me that the money isn't their end goal. They've put in the work and made sure that the product was right, that artists created great songs, and that audiences of thousands nodded their heads in unison like robots, and money has been the eventual result. Money is always a result of providing a stellar service to people.

While explaining his idea of success, Chuck adequately broke down the relationship between success and money:

> When one of your songs rocks [the] club, when one of your favorite artists rocks one of your tracks, and when one of your songs is on the radio—ain't a better feeling in the world when the radio is playing your song! None of those that I said involves money. Money comes with this territory. If you do any one of them three, money is on the way, so it's definitely not the money issue. Now at the end, I am happy and proud when I see someone going from not having to [being] able to afford their lifestyle and help out their family. [But it] still came from [one of] them three.

Those are powerful words to consider. Money is a result of a passionate and relentless focus on the craft.

Another thing to realize is that there are more paths to victory than you may be aware of. Back in '04 when I started producing, I, like many, automatically associated everything I would ever touch with major record labels. There's nothing wrong with that at all, but I made that association out of ignorance of the many roles a creator of music plays in the world. Who's producing the music under that commercial you're watching on television? What if I told you that guy is earning a great living from producing and making music for brands? Who wrote the score for the video game you're playing? Whose techno music is playing under the action sequence of that film you're streaming from Netflix? Who's behind the music of international artists? What about the rise of DJ/producers performing shows and rocking clubs with their *own* beats? Forced by the declines in the industry, many producers are just now scrambling for ways to creatively construct their careers. But some producers have been winning by thinking outside of the box for years. I just hope that you don't passively assume that you can't be successful until you get a Jay-Z record.

WHY YOU'RE REALLY HERE

Also, please stay connected to the true purpose of why we do what we do. Do it because you're absolutely crazy about it. Do it as if you were never going to receive a penny, but you just want to be excellent at your craft and you enjoy making people feel great. Do it because you love the bond you create with people's emotions. I realized at some point that the producer's product is like a drug. *You, creator of music,*

are an acute link between humans and their emotions.
That's ultimately what you're doing as you create
sound. We listen to music to feel, whether we want
to mellow out, amp up and prepare for the party, set
a sexy mood, go crazy, or curl up inside of our anger.
There's a definite, psychological connection to music.
And you create it. If you're doing all of this properly,
you're smart, and you're putting your whole self into
your creativity and your business, into manipulating
the world's emotions, the dough will come.

Says DJ Khalil,

> Success is setting out a plan and achieving those
> goals. [It's] not really money. [The] money comes
> and goes.

Needlz explains,

> For me success is for your name to be mentioned
> [with] the top cats. [I] would like to be known as
> one of the top people in my craft. Not necessarily
> the most paid, but one of the illest to do it.

If you meet the goals of leaving a legacy and being mentioned with the best, abundance will surely
be granted to you. How many of you want to leave
behind a legacy? How many of you have said to
yourself that you wanted to be honored in this game,
the way we honor legendary creators like Primo, J
Dilla, Dre, Just Blaze, Rick Rubin, or Quincy Jones?
That's a fantastic compass to follow, one with the

potential to bring you face to face with your dreams.

Also, if you've got the correct mindset programmed, the journey shouldn't have an end destination. You will constantly evolve, improve, and master your craft. You'll move from genre to genre, from music to film, from faceless producer to respected composer of music. If your goal is to actually do this for the long haul, then that's how you'll have to think. Hen says,

> It's kind of one of those things [that is] ongoing; I don't think we'll ever feel like *we made it*. I don't think we'll ever feel like we did what we needed to do because the goal is always adapting, always changing.

Keep Hen's philosophy in mind as you walk your path.

What's also interesting about production success is that you can clearly trace a direct link between someone's goals and where that person is in life. When defining success, typically, the younger you are, the more the focus tends to be on material, shiny things. The producers I've interviewed in this book, for the most part, are in their thirties and have been in, around, and making music for years. Their vision of success has evolved and matured, much like them.

Focus says,

> ...If you would've asked me this years ago, when I was really heavy in[to] trying to be a legend, then I would have said, "Being ... the best producer

and being a legend." But when you're a family man, and you look at your seeds, and you're able to provide for your seeds, they tell you they love you, and you're married and all that stuff, there's nothing in the world like it. I got a Grammy, I got Platinum plaques, I got some sort of respect in the industry and so on and so forth. I did everything that I thought I needed to do that was gonna make me happy, and it didn't bring me the happiness that my children and my wife did.

That's a grown-man response to success. I just thought it was an interesting point of view I should share with you. Make sure to stay in tune with your evolved vision of production success. It will mature as you do.

So consider all of these things about success as a producer. The passion for making great music and the desire to leave a legacy are the alchemy that turn your work into money. Remember to look outside the box for extra opportunities as well. Define victory for yourself and make it your mission. I can't wait for the day that one of you cats comes up to me and tells me that reading this work contributed to your getting where you needed to go. Then I'll get to taste my own version of success.

When you chase music for money, God walks out of the room. —Quincy Jones

MASTERING

> What people don't understand is that *you're in control*. You control what your music sounds like, who you work with. It's God and it's you. *You can achieve anything.* —DJ Khalil

It's my sincere hope that the experiences and information penned in this personal book offer valuable insight and knowledge. It's my definite purpose to provide you with a set of useful tools to help you achieve your most precious goals. With the right tools, anything can be built, and I want this book to be an important piece of your toolkit.

We never know how our path will progress or what our current pursuits will unfold to become. Looking back on my own journey, I think it's likely that I was supposed to fall in love with production, attack it for four years, and make enough grave mistakes to provide me with the experiences needed to write this book, so *you* can succeed. And all of those experiences I humbly offer to you. Many, if not all, will cross your path at some point in your journey as a producer. Remember them as you will encounter them. Remember that everything you need to win rests within that big, beautiful brain of yours. Remember that it all boils down to how you're thinking and feeling. You'll take every action you should or shouldn't, based on the conversations you're having with yourself. That's a massive responsibility, but it's yours and no one else's. It's not mine. It's not the record label's. It doesn't belong to an A&R, an artist, or a music supervisor. You are the captain of your ship. Whether you sail into the sunset of production success or crash and sink on the rocky shores of failure rests on you. Circumstances will step into your career to assist you. People will walk in and open doors for you. Opportunities will reveal themselves to you. But it rests on you to be mentally and creatively prepared when those things manifest.

I wish you the best on your track trek. The majority of the industry won't give a damn about what you're striving to become. But we're united by a passion for the same art. I want to see you win, because I know what it feels like to be insanely in love with production. This is far from an easy path to travel. But it's within your grasp to be victorious; to have your name mentioned with the greats; to evolve the sound of music; to set the standard; to reap the rewards of mastering your craft and serving the needs of thousands of music lovers; to earn respect; to leave a legacy; to inspire the next generation of aspiring producers. Many have done it before you, many are doing it now, and many will do it in the years to come. But your mind and heart must be right.

Lastly, although I've laid out many of my own disasters to avoid and joined them with successful techniques of people who are winning, nobody's journey is exactly the same. What works or doesn't work for one person isn't necessarily applicable to the next. You'll need to couple these experiences with your own trials, errors, and successes to find your own golden path. But regardless of the techniques you choose, it is still a path, and you walk it by working every day. Believe. Believe. Believe. Govern yourselves accordingly. Happy hunting.

> [That] moment between you and the music, you know, that moment where you've got the headphones on, or you've got the music playing loud and you're going through things in life and you sit down to make music to vent, to get something out—I think that there is the *purest form of creation that keeps all of us sane.* I think everyone kind of started doing it to get something out— ... therapy, in a sense. — REO, the Soundkillers

Never treat this art form with less respect than it deserves. I hold all of you in my highest regard.

—Christopher "MayDay" Rucks

CPSIA information can be obtained
at www.ICGtesting.com
Printed in the USA
BVOW09s1733070318
509943BV00029B/1799/P

9 780989 786102